THE POWER
WITHIN US

THE POWER WITHIN US

Russell M. Nelson

Deseret Book Company
Salt Lake City, Utah

No part of this book may be reproduced in any
form or by any means without permission in writing
from the publisher, Deseret Book Company,
P.O. Box 30178, Salt Lake City, Utah 84130.
Deseret Book is a registered trademark of
Deseret Book Company.

First printing September 1988
Second printing November 1988
Third printing January 1989
Fourth printing March 1989

Library of Congress Cataloging-in-Publication Data

Nelson, Russell M.
    The power within us / by Russell M. Nelson.
       p.   cm.
    Bibliography: p.
    Includes index.
    ISBN 0-87579-154-9 : $9.95 (est.)
      1. Church of Jesus Christ of Latter-day Saints — Sermons.
2. Mormon Church — Sermons. 3. Sermons, American. I. Title.
BX8639.N45P68   1988
252′.09332 — dc19   88-20299
                                                       CIP

CONTENTS

PREFACE

The older I grow, the more I appreciate the uniqueness of an individual life. Literally, no two people are alike. Each one has a specific genetic inheritance indelibly stamped upon every cell. Environmental influences from the company one keeps, and experiences that one endures, blend to enrich and educate the person who ultimately emerges from this marvelous experience we call life. If another can gain insight from my perspectives, I would feel justified in the publication of this volume.

As my name appears as author, I realize that, to a real extent, I am the product of others. From each wonderful person I have met, I have tried to acquire a measure of goodness. From the science of medicine and the discipline of surgery, I have learned the necessity of knowledge and of obedience to law if desired results are to be achieved. From sacred scriptures, I have learned divine law—the everlasting word of God—which is responsible for any component of my messages that may be timeless.

This is not an official publication of the Church. I alone am responsible and stand accountable for viewpoints expressed. As I consider the countless hours devoted to the preparation of each message, I have rendered such written effort where I am with what I have. Yet I recognize that imperfection is still apparent—a quality that is ever a part of me.

Pondering, praying, preparing, and proclaiming are important for an ordained apostle. Called by divine inspiration and revelation, he leaves the career of the world for which he has been initially educated and prayerfully submits himself to his Master, knowing that the Lord will use His servants to accomplish His will, even in their weakness. Messages that result are, in a way, comparable to letters penned earlier by Paul, John, or James. For their day and for their time, those writings represented the legacy of faith they chose to leave to their loved ones. In that spirit, this compilation of messages prepared—epistles written—is offered to those who seek the perspective of this fellow traveler among them.

In the final analysis, however, the written word is only an evidence of the real message that comprises the life of an individual. This thought I have tried to summarize in "My Message," a song I composed, the words of which are as follows:

> Our God is my Maker;
> Parents dear are my guide;
> An angel wife my true love;
> Children choice are my pride.
> Our Lord is my Light;
> His endless truth, my law.
> My joy is in service to others;
> My message is—my life.

ACKNOWLEDGMENTS

To parents, one can never adequately return appreciation, no matter how thoroughly one might try. Marion C. and Edna A. Nelson have given much more than parenthood. They have provided priceless example. Brothers, sisters, friends, and colleagues have also done much to shape my soul. To my eternal companion, Dantzel, I offer my gratitude for her unselfish partnership. Never murmuring, always enduring, she has helped me to achieve goals that once seemed so distant, almost beyond our comprehension. To our ten children, and also to their partners, whom we love as our own, I express special gratitude as well. Their children, whom we gratefully love as our grandchildren, add a special dimension of joy and, at the same time, additional feelings of responsibility. Family members have been so patient and helpful.

My secretary, Helen R. Hillier, always cheerful even through the final draft, deserves special commendation. To Eleanor Knowles, I am grateful for careful and patient editorial review.

Even with deep appreciation for the help of so many, I personally bear responsibility for the content of this volume. Shortcomings, omissions, and deficiencies compared with the talents of others are clearly mine. Things of everlasting value surely emanate from Him whose servant I am. For His help, I am humbly grateful.

Chapter 1

THE MAGNIFICENCE OF MAN

I invite you to ponder things magnificent. The word *magnificent* is derived from two Latin roots. The prefix, *magni,* comes from a term meaning "great." The suffix comes from the Latin *facere,* which means "to make" or "to do." A simple definition of *magnificent,* then, might be "great deed" or "greatly made."

Think, if you will, of the most magnificent sight you have ever seen. It could be a meadow in springtime filled with beautiful wildflowers. Or perhaps you have been awestruck, as have I, at the magnificence of a single rose with its special beauty and perfume. I have come to appreciate the magnificence of an orange, with each droplet of juice neatly packaged in an edible container, joined with many other packets, grouped in sections, and all neatly wrapped in a disposable, biodegradable peel.

Some would say that the most magnificent sight they have ever beheld is the heavens on a summer night, with stars beyond number dotting the sky. Those who have traveled in orbit through space say that their view of the planet earth has been one of the most magnificent sights ever observed by man.

Some might choose the view of the Grand Canyon at sunrise; others, the beauty of a mountain lake, river, waterfall, or desert.

Some might select a peacock with its tail in full fan, or a

1

handsome horse. Others would nominate the beauty of butterfly wings, or a hummingbird seemingly suspended in midair while feeding.

These magnificent sights are wondrous beyond measure. They are all "great deeds" of our divine Creator.

Now ponder the magnificence of all that is portrayed when you look in the mirror. Ignore the freckles, unruly hair, or blemishes, and look beyond to see the real you—a child of God—created by him, in his image. Looking beyond the surface you see in the mirror, let us lift the lid on the treasure chest of understanding of the marvelous attributes of your body and discover, at least in part, the magnificence of man. Here are some of the glittering jewels of magnificence in this treasure chest.

THE HUMAN EMBRYO

In the first compartment of the treasure chest, we might look at the magnificence of our creation itself.

We don't know precisely how two germ cells unite to become a human embryo, but we do know that both the female cell and the male cell contain all of the new individual's hereditary material and information, stored in a space so small it cannot be seen by the naked eye. Twenty-three chromosomes from both the father and the mother unite in one new cell. These chromosomes contain thousands of genes. A marvelous process of genetic coding is established by which all the basic human characteristics of the unborn person are determined. A new DNA complex is thus formed. A continuum of growth is instituted, which results in a new human being.

Approximately twenty-two days after two germ cells have united, a little heart begins to beat. At twenty-six days the circulation of blood begins. Cells multiply, divide, and become differentiated. Some become eyes that see; others, ears that hear; while still others are destined to become fingers that feel the wonderful things about us. Yes, awareness of the magnificence of man begins with the miracles of conception and our creation.

SPECIFIC ORGANS

In our treasure chest of understanding, we can look to the compartment that contains the capability of selected organs. Each jewel merits admiration, appreciation, and awe.

Let us mention first the magnificence of the eyes with which we see. No doubt you have stood before the mirror, as have I, and watched the pupils of your eyes react to changes in the intensity of light, dilating to let in more light and constricting to reduce the light allowed to reach the sensitive retina of the eye. A self-focusing lens is at the front of each eye. Nerves and muscles synchronize the function of two separate eyes to produce one three-dimensional image. Eyes are connected to the brain, ready to record sights seen. No cords, no batteries, no external connections are needed; our visual apparatus is marvelous — infinitely more priceless than any camera that money can buy.

While we may admire good stereophonic equipment for sensing sound, ponder by comparison the magnificence of the human ear. It is truly remarkable. Compacted into an area about the size of a marble is all the equipment needed to perceive sound. A tiny tympanic membrane serves as the diaphragm. Minute ossicles amplify the signal, which is then transmitted along nerve lines to the brain, which registers the result of hearing. This marvelous sound system is also connected to the recording instrument of the brain.

A large portion of my life's study and research has been focused on the jewel of the human heart — a pump that is so magnificent that its power is almost beyond our comprehension. To control the direction of flow of blood within it, there are four important valves, pliable as a parachute and delicate as a silk scarf. They open and close more than 100,000 times a day — over 36 million times a year. Yet, unless altered by disease, they are so rugged that they stand this kind of wear seemingly indefinitely. No man-made material developed thus far can be flexed this frequently and for so long without breaking.

The amount of work done by the heart is truly amazing. Each day it pumps enough fluid to fill a 2,000-gallon tank car. The work it performs daily is equivalent to lifting a 150-pound man to the top of the Empire State Building, while consuming only about four watts of energy—less than that used by a small light bulb.

At the crest of the heart is an electrical generator that transmits energy down special lines, causing myriads of muscle fibers to beat in coordination and in rhythm. This synchrony would be the envy of the conductor of any orchestra.

All this power is condensed in this faithful pump—the human heart—about the size of one's fist, energized from within by an endowment from on high.

One of the most wondrous of all jewels in this treasure chest is the human brain with its intricate combination of power cells, recording, memory, storage, and retrieval systems. It serves as headquarters for the personality and character of each human being. As I observe the lives of great individuals, I sense that the capacity of the brain is seemingly infinite. Wise men can become even wiser as each experience builds upon previous experience. Indeed, continuing exercise of the intellect brings forth increased intellectual capacity.

While I marvel at a computer and admire the work it can do, I respect even more the mind of man, which developed the computer. The human brain is certainly a recording instrument that will participate in our judgment one day when we stand before the Lord. The Book of Mormon speaks of a "bright recollection" (Alma 11:43) and of a "perfect remembrance" (Alma 5:18) that will be with us at that time. Each one of us carries that recording instrument guarded within the vault of the human skull.

As we symbolically sift through the treasure chest of understanding, we could spend hours, even a lifetime, studying the incredible chemical capacity of the liver, the kidneys, and

4

any or all of the endocrine and exocrine glands of the body. Each is a shimmering jewel, worthy of our study and our deepest gratitude.

OTHER JEWELS

Now let us turn our attention to jewels in another compartment in the treasure chest of understanding, as we consider some concepts that bridge beyond individual organ systems.

1. The first concept is that of *reserve, or backup*. In the theater, major actors often have understudies for backup. In electrical instruments, backup in the event of power failure may be provided by batteries. In the body, backup is provided by a number of organs that are paired, such as eyes, ears, lungs, adrenal glands, kidneys, and more. In the event of illness, injury, or loss of one of these organs, the other is ready to keep our bodily functions intact. In the event of loss of sight or hearing altogether, other sensory powers become augmented in a miraculous manner.

Some backup systems are not so apparent. For example, crucial single organs, such as the brain, the heart, and the liver, have a double blood supply. They are all nourished by two routes of circulation, which minimize damage in the event of loss of blood flow through any single blood vessel.

Another dimension of backup I shall describe as *collateral pathways*. For example, if your nasal passageways are obstructed by a "stuffy nose," you may breathe through your mouth. Similarly, collateral pathways may grow if blood vessels or nerves are obstructed or severed.

2. Consider another concept, that of *self-defense* of the body. One day I watched some three-year-old children lapping water from the sidewalk after it had overflowed through a neighbor's garden. I suppose the germs they ingested were incalculable in number, but not one of those children became ill. They were defended by their bodies. As soon as that dirty drink reached their stomachs, hydrochloric acid went to work to

purify the water and protect the lives of those innocent children.

Think of the protection provided by the skin. Could you make, or even conjure in your mind how to create, a cloak that would protect you and, at the same time, would warn against injuries from excessive heat or cold? That is what the skin does. It even gives signals indicating that another part of the body is ailing. The skin can flush and sweat with fever. When a person is frightened or ill, the skin pales. When one is embarrassed, the skin blushes. And it is replete with nerve fibers that communicate and often limit possible harm through perception of pain.

Pain itself is part of the body's defense mechanism. For example, sensory areas of the mouth guard and protect the esophagus, which is very delicate and has few nerve fibers. Like a sentinel, the mouth receives warnings if drinks are too hot and protects the esophagus from becoming burned.

The body's defenses include chemical antibodies that are manufactured in response to infections. Each time a person is exposed to a bacterial or viral infection, the body produces antibodies that not only combat that infection but also persist with memory to strengthen resistance in days to come. When military conscription was required in World War II, soldiers who had come from isolated rural areas had much less immunity and were more prone to infections than were those who had come from more highly populated urban areas and whose resistance was subsequently better developed.

3. Closely related to the concept of self-defense is that of *self-repair*. Consider the fact that broken bones mend and become strong once again. If we were to break one of the legs of a chair, how long would we have to wait for that chair leg to heal itself? It would never happen. Yet many people today walk on legs that once were broken. Lacerations in the skin heal themselves. A leak in the circulation will seal itself, a power that circulatory systems outside the body do not have. I gained appreciation for this fact early in my research career while

working in the laboratory to create an artifical heart-lung machine. Whenever tubing in that machine would spring a leak, I could count on spending long hours cleaning up the lab and coming home late for dinner. Never did a leak in the artificial heart-lung machine ever seal itself.

4. Another remarkable concept is that of *self-renewal.* Each cell in the body is created and then regenerated from elements of the earth according to the recipe or formula contained within genes unique to the individual. The average red blood corpuscle, for example, lives about 120 days, then dies and is replaced by another. Each time we bathe, thousands of dead and dying cells are scrubbed away, to be replaced by a younger crop. I believe that this process of self-renewal prefigures the process of resurrection.

5. Also in our treasure chest is the concept of *auto-regulation.* Have you ever wondered why you can't swim under water very long? Auto-regulation limits the time you can hold your breath. As breath is held, carbon dioxide accumulates. Partial pressure of carbon dioxide is monitored continuously by two carotid bodies in the neck, which transmit signals up nerves to the brain. The brain then sends stimuli to muscles of respiration, causing them to work, so that we might inhale a new refreshment of oxygen and eliminate retained carbon dioxide.

And have you ever wondered why you can tolerate extremes of hot and cold weather? In spite of wide fluctuations in the temperature of man's environment, the temperature of each person's body is carefully controlled within certain very narrow bounds.

These are but two of many, many servo-mechanisms that auto-regulate individual ingredients in our bodies. The number of these systems exceeds our ability to enumerate them. Sodium, potassium, water, glucose, protein, nitrogen are but a few of the many constituents continuously monitored by chemical regulators within our bodies.

6. Consider now the concept of *adaptation.* People on the

earth dwell amidst climatic and dietary differences of vast scope. Eskimos in the Arctic Circle consume a diet with a large component of fat, which is acceptable and even necessary to sustain life in a very cold climate. Polynesians, on the other hand, eat a diet provided by a tropical environment. Yet these different groups work and adapt to varying conditions and diet available to them.

7. The concept of *identity* in reproduction is marvelous to contemplate. Each of us possesses seeds that carry our unique chromosomes, and genes that help determine specific cellular identity for our children. For this reason, tissues surgically transplanted from one person to another can survive only by suppressing the host's immune response, which clearly recognizes tissues foreign to one's own inherited genetic formula. Truly we are blessed with power to have children born in the likeness of parents.

AN INTERESTING PARADOX

As we consider self-defense, self-repair, and self-renewal, an interesting paradox emerges. Limitless life could result if these marvelous qualities of the body continued in perpetuity. If we could create anything that could defend itself, repair itself, and renew itself without limit, we could create perpetual life. That is what our Creator did with the bodies he created for Adam and Eve in the Garden of Eden. Had they continued to be nourished from the tree of life, they would have lived forever. According to the Lord, as revealed through his prophets, the fall of Adam instituted the aging process, which results ultimately in physical death. Of course, we do not understand all the chemistry, but we are witnesses of the consequences of growing old. This and other pathways of release assure that there is a limit to the length of life upon the earth.

Yes, troubles do develop in bodies that do not repair themselves with time. To the skilled physician, this profound question is posed by each sick patient seen: Will this illness get better, or will it get worse, with the passage of time? The former needs only supportive care. The latter requires significant help to convert the process of progressive deterioration to one that might improve with time.

When death comes, it generally seems to the mortal mind to be untimely. At such times we need to have the larger view that death is part of life. Alma tells us, "It was not expedient that man should be reclaimed from this temporal death, for that would destroy the great plan of happiness." (Alma 42:8; see also D&C 29:43.)

When severe illness or tragic injuries claim an individual in the flowering prime of life, we can take comfort in this fact: the very laws that could not allow life to persist here are the same eternal laws that will be implemented at the time of the resurrection, when that body "shall be restored to [its] proper and perfect frame." (Alma 40:23.)

OUR DIVINE CREATION

Thoughts of life, death, and resurrection bring us to face crucial questions. How were we made? By whom? And why?

Through the ages, some persons without scriptural understanding have tried to explain our existence by pretentious words such as *ex nihilo* (out of nothing). Others have deduced that, because of certain similarities between different forms of life, there has been a natural selection of the species, or organic evolution from one form to another. Still others have concluded that man came as a consequence of a "big bang," which resulted in the creation of our planet and life upon it.

To me, such theories are unbelievable. Could an explosion in a printing shop produce a dictionary? It's unthinkable! One might argue that it is within a remote realm of possibility, but even if that could happen, such a dictionary could certainly not heal its own torn pages, renew its own worn corners, or reproduce its own subsequent editions.

We are children of God, created by him and formed in his image. Recently I studied the scriptures simply to find how many times they testify of the divine creation of man. Looking

9

up references that referred to either *create* or *form* (or their derivatives) with *man* (or such derivatives as *men, male, woman,* or *female*) in the same verse, I found that at least fifty-five verses of scripture attest to our divine creation. I have selected one to represent all those verses that convey the same conclusion: "The Gods took counsel among themselves and said: Let us go down and form man in our image, after our likeness. . . . So the Gods went down to organize man in their own image, in the image of the Gods to form they him, male and female to form they them." (Abraham 4:26-27.)

I believe all of those scriptures pertaining to the creation of man. But the decision to believe is a spiritual one, not born solely by an understanding of things physical: "The natural man receiveth not the things of the Spirit of God: for they are foolishness unto him: neither can he know them, because they are spiritually discerned." (1 Corinthians 2:14.)

It is incumbent upon each informed and spiritually attuned person to help overcome such foolishness of those who would deny divine creation or think that mankind simply evolved. By the spirit, we perceive the truer and more believable wisdom of God.

With great conviction I add my testimony to that of my fellow apostle Paul, who said: "Know ye not that ye are the temple of God, and that the Spirit of God dwelleth in you? If any man defile the temple of God, him shall God destroy; for the temple of God is holy, which temple ye are." (1 Corinthians 3:16-17.)

The Lord said that "the spirit and the body are the soul of man." (D&C 88:15.) Each of us, therefore, is a dual being—a biological (physical) entity and an intellectual (spiritual) entity. The combination of both is intimate throughout mortality.

In the beginning, man, as that intellectual entity, was with God. Our intelligence was not created or made, nor can it be. (See D&C 93:29.)

That spirit, joined with a physical body of such remarkable qualities, becomes a living soul of supernal worth. The psalmist so expressed this thought: "When I consider thy heavens, the work of thy fingers, the moon and the stars, which thou hast ordained; what is man, that thou art mindful of him? . . . For thou hast made him a little lower than the angels, and hast crowned him with glory and honour." (Psalm 8:3-5.)

Why were we created? Why are we here? Why are we upon the earth?

God has made it plain over and over again that the world was made for mankind to exist. We are here to work out our divine destiny, according to an eternal plan presented to us in the great council of heaven. Our bodies have been created to accommodate our spirits, to allow us to experience the challenges of mortality.

With this understanding, it is pure sacrilege to let anything enter the body that might defile this physical temple of God. It is irreverent to let even the gaze of our precious eyesight, or the sensors of our touch or hearing, supply the brain with memories that are unclean or unworthy.

Could any of us lightly regard precious seeds of reproduction—specifically and uniquely ours—or disregard the moral laws of God, who gave divine rules governing their sacred use?

Knowing we are created as children of God, and that he has given us agency to choose, we must also know that we are accountable to him. He has defined the truth and has prescribed commandments. Obedience to his law brings us joy. Disobedience of those commandments is defined as sin. While we live in a world that seems increasingly reluctant to designate dishonorable deeds as sinful, a scripture warns us: "Fools make a mock at sin: but among the righteous there is favour." (Proverbs 14:9.)

No one is perfect. Some may have sinned grievously in transgressing God's laws. Mercifully, we can repent. That is an important part of life's opportunity, as well.

Repentance requires spiritual dominion over appetites of the flesh. Every physical system has appetite. Our desires to eat, drink, see, hear, and feel respond to those appetites. But all appetites must be controlled by the intellect in order for us to attain true joy. On the other hand, whenever we allow uncontrolled appetites of the body to determine behavior opposed to nobler promptings of the Spirit, the stage is set for misery and grief.

Such substances as alcohol, tobacco, and harmful drugs are forbidden by the Lord. We have similarly been warned about the evils of pornography and unclean thoughts. Appetites for these degrading forces can become addictive. Physical or mental addictions become doubly serious because, in time, they enslave both the body and the spirit. Full repentance from these shackles, or any other yokes to sin, must be accomplished in this life, while we still have the aid of a mortal body to help us develop self-mastery.

When we truly know our divine nature, our thoughts and behavior will be more appropriate. Then we will control our appetites. We will focus our eyes on sights, our ears on sounds, and our minds on thoughts that are a credit to our physical creation as a temple of our Father in heaven.

In daily prayer, we may gratefully acknowledge God as our Creator, thank him for the magnificence of our physical temple, and then heed his counsel.

MORE YET TO LEARN

Though we cannot fully comprehend the magnificence of man, in faith we can continue our reverent quest. We may join with Jacob in this marvelous declaration: "Behold, great and marvelous are the works of the Lord. How unsearchable are the depths of the mysteries of him; and it is impossible that man should find out all his ways. . . . For behold, by the power of his word man came upon the face of the earth, which earth was created by the power of his word. . . . Therefore, brethren, seek not to counsel the Lord, but to take counsel from his hand." (Jacob 4:8-10.)

For years I have attended scientific meetings of learned

societies. Medical scientists and practitioners by the thousands participate in such assemblies annually from all over the world. The quest for knowledge is endless. It seems that the more we know, the more there is yet to learn. It is impossible that any of us may learn all the ways of God. But as we are faithful and are deeply rooted in scriptural accounts of God's magnificent creations, we will be well prepared for future discoveries. All truth is compatible because it all emanates from God.

Of course, we know that "there is an opposition in all things." (2 Nephi 2:11.) In the world even many so-called "educators" teach contrary to divine truth. Be mindful of this prophetic counsel: "O the vainness, and the frailties, and the foolishness of men! When they are learned they think they are wise, and they hearken not unto the counsel of God, for they set it aside, supposing they know of themselves, wherefore, their wisdom is foolishness and it profiteth them not. And they shall perish. But to be learned is good if they hearken unto the counsels of God." (2 Nephi 9:28-29.)

We need not be reminded that the work and glory of the Lord are opposed by forces of Satan, who is the master of deceit. Many follow his teachings. Remember, "Man may deceive his fellow-men, deception may follow deception, and the children of the wicked one may have power to seduce the foolish and untaught, till naught but fiction feeds the many, and the fruit of falsehood carries in its current the giddy to the grave." (JS-History 1:71, footnote.)

Be wise and keep away from temptations and snares. Cautiously avoid "foolish and hurtful lusts, which drown men in destruction and perdition. . . . Flee these things; and follow after righteousness, godliness, faith, love, patience, meekness. Fight the good fight of faith, lay hold on eternal life." (1 Timothy 6:9, 11-12.)

OUR ETERNAL SPIRIT

The magnificence of man is matchless. Remember, glorious as this physical tabernacle is, the body is designed to support

13

something even more glorious — the eternal spirit that dwells in the mortal frame of each of us. The great accomplishments of this life are rarely physical. Those attributes by which we shall be judged one day are spiritual. With the blessing of our bodies to assist us, we may develop spiritual qualities of honesty, integrity, compassion, and love. Only with the development of the spirit may we acquire "faith, virtue, knowledge, temperance, patience, brotherly kindness, godliness, charity, humility, [and] diligence." (D&C 4:6.)

May we pattern our lives after our great Exemplar, even Jesus the Christ, whose parting words among mankind included this eternal challenge: "What manner of men ought ye to be? . . . even as I am." (3 Nephi 27:27.) We are sons and daughters of God. He is our Father; we are his children. Our divine inheritance is the magnificence of man.

Chapter 2

THREE STEPS TOWARD
A MONUMENTAL LIFE

In the summer of 1986 a major focus of attention in the United States was the Statue of Liberty on her hundredth anniversary and the celebration of her remodeling. While most monuments are erected to people or specific events, this one is indeed unique. Lady Liberty commemorates an ideal. But this and other monuments can also teach us important lessons about life.

Those lessons are embraced in the words of the hymn "I'll Go Where You Want Me to Go." (*Hymns*, no. 270.) Within its text are several powerful commitments to action, including I'll go (where you want me to go), I'll do (thy will with a heart sincere), and I'll be (what you want me to be). By applying these concepts to personal development, each of us can help build a monumental life. Through the process of becoming, we may go, do, and be a living monument.

A monument requires a base to support the vertical shaft of its statement. The Statue of Liberty has a splendid eighty-nine-foot pedestal erected on a sixty-five-foot star-shaped base.

A monumental life also begins with a broad base of understanding. Three steps in the process of forging a monumental life from its base are neatly tucked in the verses of our song: I'll go, I'll do, I'll be. These three statements comprise the outline of my message.

15

I'LL GO

Step one is "I'll go." But before we go anywhere, it is well to consider where we have been. Life's journey did not start with our first mortal breath. Prior to our birth, we were with God as his spirit children. We walked with him, talked with him, and knew him. We each shouted for joy with the prospects of a journey to earth to gain a physical body and to experience unique challenges here. I suspect we were terrified, at first, when told we would forget Father, friends, and facts we formerly knew so well. I can believe we were calmed when informed that our Father in heaven would provide prophets and scriptures to guide us and a means whereby we could communicate with him through prayer and the spirit of revelation. Still, we may have been a bit insecure when we learned that faith — faith to believe the intangible — was the key to success in our journey. Faith was to be the critical component in our safe return to our Father in heaven. Few have had better insight than did Abraham, who recorded:

> Now the Lord had shown unto me, Abraham, the intelligences that were organized before the world was; and among all these there were many of the noble and great ones;
> And God saw these souls that they were good, and he stood in the midst of them, and he said: These I will make my rulers; for he stood among those that were spirits, and he saw that they were good; and he said unto me: Abraham, thou art one of them; thou wast chosen before thou wast born.
> And there stood one among them that was like unto God, and he said unto those who were with him: We will go down, for there is space there, and we will take of these materials, and we will make an earth whereon these may dwell;
> And we will prove them herewith, to see if they will do all things whatsoever the Lord their God shall command them. (Abraham 3:22-25.)

Once here, the journey through life for each of us may include other travels in order to meet our personal rendezvous with destiny. Father Lehi and Mother Sariah departed from the wealth and security of Jerusalem and trekked for many days

16

across hot desert sands to the eastern shores of the Red Sea. Then Lehi asked his sons to return to Jerusalem to get the brass plates of Laban. What did that assignment entail?

If we were to compare that to Utah and our situation today, we would have to walk a distance equivalent to that from Provo to St. George, Utah, approximately three hundred miles, across scorching sand, with no freeways, no air conditioning, no cold drinks. Then we would be asked to walk all the way back to Provo, tackle a tough assignment, and walk back to St. George. No wonder Laman and Lemuel murmured! That was the setting for this matchless statement of Nephi: "I will go and do the things which the Lord hath commanded, for I know that the Lord giveth no commandments unto the children of men, save he shall prepare a way for them that they may accomplish the thing which he commandeth them." (1 Nephi 3:7.)

Nephi and his brothers eventually returned with the brass plates. Even Sariah had complained when her sons were required to make this long, hazardous journey. Shortly thereafter, Lehi told his sons to return once again to Jerusalem, this time to get Ishmael and his family. Perhaps each young man felt a bit better about it this time, knowing that there was the possibility he might be rewarded with one of the daughters of Ishmael to become his wife. This rugged discipline was but a prologue to Lehi's family's going subsequently all the way across what we now know as the Saudi Arabian Peninsula to its southeastern shore, where ships were to be built. And this challenge was but prelude to their ultimate destiny—to go across ocean waters to the promised land.

In fact, much of scriptural history reports requirements of the Lord's prophets and people to go to their particular proving grounds.

For David, his destiny with Goliath required that he go to the valley of Elah. (See 1 Samuel 17:19.)

Moses had to go to the heights of Sinai and to the depths of the Red Sea, whose waters had been parted by the power of the priesthood he bore. (See Alma 36:28.)

Joseph Smith, Brigham Young, and our early pioneer predecessors had to go from the eastern extremity of the United States to Ohio, Missouri, and Illinois and then across a hostile environment to "the mountain of the Lord's house" in the top of the mountains (see Isaiah 2:2; 2 Nephi 12:2), to a place we now know as world headquarters of the Lord's church.

All eight of my great-grandparents, individually converted to the Church in populous nations of Europe, had to leave their family and the comforts of home to go this new land and across its challenging terrain, eventually settling in the little town of Ephraim, Utah.

Each of us will have to go to unique testing grounds of faith. For some it may be abroad, or on missions, for preparation or assignment far beyond comforts of home, family, and friends. For others, particularly busy young mothers and fathers, their appointment with destiny is within the walls of home. Their enemy is neither the hot sands of the desert nor smoking guns of foes in pursuit, but heated efforts of the adversary to undermine their marriage and/or the sanctity of the family unit. For the monument of their life to rise from its pedestal of preparation to their appointed site of destiny, they must go where the Lord wants them to go. Wherever it is, each of us must go with the same faith that allowed us to leave our heavenly home in the first place.

I'LL DO

Step two is "I'll Do." These words remind me of the development of the song "I Am a Child of God." When lyricist Naomi W. Randall first composed the words to this hymn, they read, "Teach me all that I must know, to live with Him some day." Before he became president of the Church, President Spencer W. Kimball suggested that the word *know* be changed to *do.* In explaining why he wanted the change, he said, "To know isn't enough. The devils know and tremble; the devils know everything. We have to *do* something." (*Church News,* April 1, 1978, p. 16; emphasis added.)

18

As President Kimball implied, some foes of righteousness may actually know more than many of us. To know isn't enough. Even today, some very knowledgeable physicians still smoke cigarettes. They know better. Some Latter-day Saints who know about such divine laws as chastity, tithing, or honesty experience difficulty in doing what the law requires.

There are more things to do in life than time available in which to do them. That means choices need to be made. Choices are often facilitated by asking well-focused questions. Some may be thoughtfully tendered in prayer. Joseph Smith recorded his question: "My object in going to inquire of the Lord was to know which of all the sects was right, that I might know which to join." The unexpected answer: "Join none of them." (JS–History 1:18-19.)

Such a question, asked with determination beforehand to do whatever is learned, will bring heavenly direction. For example, near the end of the Book of Mormon is this challenge: "If ye shall ask with a sincere heart, with real intent [meaning you intend to *do*], . . . he will manifest the truth of it unto you." (Moroni 10:4.) Intent is an important part of the formula that precedes testimony, which brought many of us into the Church.

How did we get the Word of Wisdom? Joseph Smith first asked an important question. In answer to fervent prayer with intent to do the revealed will of the Lord, he received section 89 of the Doctrine and Covenants by revelation.

What preceded the vision of the redemption of the dead? President Joseph F. Smith pondered, not just read, the writings of Peter. (See D&C 138:1-5.) Pondering the scriptures is done with an inquiring mind.

What predated the revelation on the priesthood received by President Spencer W. Kimball in 1978? Extended meditation and intelligent inquiry, prayerfully posed in the holy temple.

Before we can start to *do*, we must ask, "What do I want to do?" Then we may properly select those activities that will help us do the things that are uniquely ours to do. That question involves our purpose and our destiny.

Can you summarize the goal of your life and state it in a simple sentence as did the Savior? He said, "My work and my glory—[is] to bring to pass the immortality and eternal life of man." (Moses 1:39.)

Counsel from President Joseph F. Smith was concisely stated: "The important consideration is ... how well we can ... discharge our duties and obligations to God and to one another." (*Gospel Doctrine*, p. 270.)

Should that concept not be part of our greatest goal, if we truly believe in God and believe that we are his children and are preparing to return to him? And if it truly is our objective, can there be any action appropriate for us to do other than to keep his commandments?

This was the plea of the Savior, who reported, "Not every one that saith unto me, Lord, Lord, shall enter into the kingdom of heaven; but he that doeth the will of my Father which is in heaven." (Matthew 7:21.) Another writer so recorded this inquiry: "Why call ye me, Lord, Lord, and do not the things which I say?" (Luke 6:46.) James admonished: "Be ye doers of the word, and not hearers only." (James 1:22.) King Benjamin also confirmed this concept. He said, "If you believe all these things see that ye do them." (Mosiah 4:10.)

If the most important things in life are to know God and to keep his commandments, then heeding his prophets and abiding their teachings should be among our most important objectives. In a way, the very repetition of the teachings of prophets may have sounded monotonous throughout the years. The pleadings of Abraham, Isaac, Jacob, Moses, and Abinadi have not differed significantly from those of President Harold B. Lee, President Spencer W. Kimball, or President Ezra Taft Benson. Surely when measured by eternal standards, teachings of the prophets are more important and enduring than the latest findings of competent researchers, even if these findings are both discovered and taught by use of modern technology and teaching aids. Success is determined largely by individual desire to learn. When we crave learning as much as we want to satisfy pangs of hunger, we will achieve our desired objectives.

I was with Elder Mark E. Petersen in the Holy Land in October 1983, during his last mortal journey. Elder Petersen was not well. Evidences of his consuming malignancy were painfully real to him, yet he derived strength from the Savior he served. Following a night of intense suffering, exacerbated by pangs of his progressive inability to eat or to drink, Elder Petersen addressed throngs assembled at the Mount of the Beatitudes to hear his discourse on the Sermon on the Mount. After he recited "Blessed are they which do hunger and thirst after righteousness," he departed from the biblical text and pleaded this question: "Do you know what it is to be really hungry? Do you know what it is to really be thirsty? Do you desire righteousness as you would desire food under extreme conditions or drink under extreme conditions? [The Savior] expects us to literally hunger and thirst after righteousness and seek it with all our hearts!"

I was one of the few present on that occasion who knew how hungry and thirsty Elder Petersen really was. His encroaching cancer had deprived him of relief from physical hunger and thirst, so he understood that doctrine. He withstood the trial. He thanked the Lord, who lent him power to preach his last major sermon at the sacred site where Jesus himself had preached.

Counsel was given by another prophet, Jacob, who said, "Feast upon that which perisheth not, neither can be corrupted." (2 Nephi 9:51.)

Nephi declared: "If ye shall press forward, feasting upon the word of Christ, and endure to the end, . . . ye shall have eternal life." (2 Nephi 31:20.) Even though Elder Petersen had been deprived of full physical feeding, he continued to feast upon the words of his Savior. He endured to the end, and I know he earned that promised reward.

To facilitate your feast, may I share a personal pattern of scriptural study that may also be helpful to you? I have marked my LDS edition of the King James Version of the Bible to highlight enrichment material from three alternate translations. I have colored those little letters above the biblical text that draw attention to corresponding footnotes below, which I have also marked with colored dots. Those citations from Hebrew, I have marked with blue circles over both the cross-referenced superscript letter and the corresponding footnote entry below. The Old Testament comes to us primarily from the Hebrew or languages closely associated with Hebrew.

The New Testament comes to us primarily from the Greek. Thus, the alternate translation from the Greek often adds significantly to a better understanding of the New Testament. The little superscript letters and corresponding footnotes from Greek, I have marked with green dots.

For passages clarified by excerpts from the Joseph Smith Translation of the Bible, I have marked the superscript letters and corresponding footnote citations with red dots.

Now whenever I turn to a page of scripture, I can immediately spot special insights provided by this enrichment material. Importance of these enhancements was taught by the Prophet Joseph Smith, who said, "Our latitude and longitude can be determined in the original Hebrew with far greater accuracy than in the English version." (*Teachings of the Prophet Joseph Smith*, p. 290.)

I'LL BE

"To be" involves the process of becoming. The word *becoming* appears in the standard works in only nine verses of scripture. Two of those references pertain to the Lord's becoming who he was. (See Mosiah 15:3, 7.) A third verse pertains to the mortal body and its becoming spiritual and immortal at the time of the resurrection. (See Alma 11:45.)

All six remaining verses employing this word refer to the ongoing battle of the flesh becoming subject to the spirit. We feel this every day as carnal temptations of the flesh contend

22

with our deeper desire for spiritual supremacy. (See Mosiah 15:5; 16:3; 27:25; Alma 12:31; 13:28; Helaman 3:16.)

In this real world of carnal competition for our fidelity, the process of becoming necessarily involves self-mastery— supremacy of the spirit over appetites of the flesh.

Our hymn tells us, "I'll be what you want me to be." Question: What does the Lord really want you and me to be? He has given us the answer definitely and repeatedly. In the Sermon on the Mount he taught his disciples, "Be ye therefore perfect, even as your Father which is in heaven is perfect." My little red dot at this quotation from Matthew 5:48 draws attention to the footnote, where I find an even stronger statement from the Joseph Smith Translation: "Ye are therefore *commanded* to be perfect, even as your Father which is in heaven is perfect." (JST, Matthew 5:50; emphasis added.)

To his disciples in the Western Hemisphere, the resurrected Lord proclaimed this divine injunction: "I would that ye should be perfect even as I, or your Father who is in heaven is perfect." (3 Nephi 12:48.)

How do we explain these similar but meaningfully different statements? Between the time of his Sermon on the Mount and his sermon to the Nephites, the sinless Savior had become perfected by his atonement. *Perfect* comes from the Greek word *teleios*, meaning "complete," and is derived from the Greek word *telos*, which connotes "to set out for a definite point or goal." It conveys the concept of conclusion of an act. Therefore, *perfect* in Matthew 5:48 also means "finished," "completed," "consummated," or "fully developed," and refers to the reality of the glorious resurrection of our Master.

Before his crucifixion, Jesus taught, "Behold, I cast out devils, and I do cures to day and to morrow, and the third day I shall be perfected." (Luke 13:32.)

His atonement provides that the body, once corruptible, now may become incorruptible. Our physical frame, once capable of death and decay, may now become immortal and beyond crumbling deterioration. That body presently sustained by the blood of life (see Leviticus 17:11) and ever changing may one day become sustained by spirit—changeless and incapable of death anymore.

Thus, the admonition to be perfect should not cause depression among us. To the contrary, it should bring us great joy and jubilation. The Lord knew that the procedure would be long and challenging, so he added this word of encouragement: "For verily I say unto you, they [the best gifts] are given for the benefit of those who love me and keep my commandments, and him that *seeketh so to do;* that all may be benefited." (D&C 46:9; emphasis added.) Those who are really seeking to do his will are recipients of his blessings, for he knows the intent of our hearts.

As he concluded his ministry among the Nephites, Jesus issued this powerful challenge: "What manner of men ought ye to be? Verily I say unto you, even as I am." (3 Nephi 27:27.)

These two words, "I am," the simplest words in all scripture, appear in the New Testament in the Greek language as ἐγώ εἰμι, which may be pronounced as *ego eimi.* In the original text of the Old Testament, "I am" is read in Hebrew as היה, which may be pronounced *hayah.*

Let our jargonal journey begin with John 8:58. Inquisitors once asked Jesus if he had seen Abraham. "Jesus said unto them, Verily, verily, I say unto you, Before Abraham was, I am." (In the Greek text these two special words are *ego eimi.*)

My green dotted mark at superscript *b* before "I am" refers me to a green dotted footnote: "John 58*b* The term I AM used here in the Greek is identical with the Septuagint usage in Ex. 3:14 which identifies Jehovah."

So, let us cross-refer back to Exodus 3 and look for clarification. The scene is on Mount Sinai. A dialogue is taking place between Moses and the Lord. I presume Moses was suffering some kind of identity crisis (at verse 11) when he said unto God:

> Who am I, that I should go unto Pharaoh, and that I should bring forth the children of Israel out of Egypt?

24

And he said, Certainly I will be with thee; and this shall be a token unto thee, that I have sent thee: When thou hast brought forth the people out of Egypt, ye shall serve God upon this mountain.

And Moses said unto God, Behold, when I come unto the children of Israel, and shall say unto them, The God of your fathers hath sent me unto you; and they shall say to me, What is his name? what shall I say unto them?

And God said unto Moses, I AM THAT I AM: and he said, Thus shalt thou say unto the children of Israel, I AM hath sent me unto you. (Exodus 3:11-14.)

In the Hebrew language of the Old Testament, "I am" comes from the word *hayah*. Translated into English, it means "to be," or "existence," and applies as well to the future as it does to the present tense. Indeed, this verse could be translated, "I will become what I will become." Here, to Moses the premortal Messiah is not only proclaiming one of His names, but also choosing a word that could literally imply the redeeming role He was yet destined to fulfill.

Two other facts about the word *hayah* are of interest:

1. *Hayah* is the Hebrew root from which the word "Jehovah" is derived.

2. It is closely related to the Hebrew term *havah*, and shares in common two of three characters הוה. *Havah* means "to be," as does *hayah*, but it also has the connotation "to breathe."

Are there hints hidden in the deep meaning of God's reply, recorded in Exodus 3:14? We know the treasured truths that the Lord God Jehovah, creator of heaven and earth under the direction of the Father, revealed to Moses one of the Lord's special names. This word may have intimated his role in the eternal existence of man, including the inception of the breath of life into his nostrils, to man's potential immortality. All this was to be made possible through the atoning sacrifice for which he, Jesus the Christ, was to be sent to the earth to effect.

Now let us look at selected verses of the New Testament. First, Mark 14:61-62: "Again the high priest asked him, and said unto him, Art thou the Christ, the Son of the Blessed? And Jesus said, I am." Next, John 4:25-26: "The woman saith unto him, I know that Messias cometh, which is called Christ: when he is come, he will tell us all things. Jesus saith unto her, I that speak unto thee am he."

In the King James Version, the last word of that verse, *he*, is printed in italics, meaning that King James translators added that word for clarification of meaning. In the Greek text, the sentence contains these two words: *ego eimi* (I am). The words of Jesus in this passage could be translated "I am [is] speaking to you."

Let us turn next to John 8:28: "Then said Jesus unto them, When ye have lifted up the Son of man, then shall ye know that I am he, and that I do nothing of myself; but as my Father hath taught me, I speak these things." Here again, King James translators added the word *he* after "I am" and italicized it to note their honest addition. But the Greek New Testament records: "Then shall ye know that *ego eimi* (I am)."

Yes, before Abraham was, Jesus was "I am"— *hayah* in Hebrew or *ego eimi* in Greek. Under the Father's plan, Jehovah—Creator, God of this world, Savior and Redeemer—was indeed "The Great I Am." Although the phrase "The Great I Am" does not appear in the text of the King James Version of the Bible, it is evident that the Prophet Joseph Smith understood this concept well. Three times he recorded this wording in the Doctrine and Covenants, in the first verse of sections 29, 38, and 39.

I'll conclude our scriptural sojourn by returning to the challenge of Jesus to us: "What manner of men ought ye to be? . . . even as I am." (3 Nephi 27:27.)

May we each be inspired by such an example and by great monuments, consider our living a monumental life, enlarge our pedestal of preparation, and then ultimately build on these three steps:

1. *I'll go*. I'll go with faith to the arena of life's challenge.

2. *I'll do*. I'll do whatever I can to erect a shaft of righteous endeavor that will remain even beyond my days.

3. *I'll be.* And "be not weary in well doing" (Galatians 6:9; 2 Thessalonians 3:13), but "let them that suffer according to the will of God commit the keeping of their souls to him in well doing, as unto a faithful Creator" (1 Peter 4:19).

May we not be discouraged when imperfections of ourselves and of our loved ones seem more than we can bear. The Lord has told us, "Continue in patience until ye are perfected." (D&C 67:13.) Then we may be, as the Lord pleaded, "even as I am." We will be numbered among his elect and will be known of him at the glorious advent of his Second Coming. "There is no other way or means whereby man can be saved, only in and through Christ. Behold, he is the life and the light of the world. Behold, he is the word of truth and righteousness." (Alma 38:9.)

By so learning and living, our lives will become monumental, not only as a tribute to our own accomplishments, but also as an everlasting credit to him who created us. God bless us to go where he wants us to go, to do his will with a heart sincere, and to be what he wants us to be.

Chapter 3

BEGIN WITH THE END
IN MIND

What would you like said about you at your funeral? Or if you were to write your own eulogy and you could have only three sentences (no big flowery speeches, please), what would you want to say?

If I were to write what I hope might be said about me, those three sentences would include:

1. I was able to render service of worth to my fellowmen.

2. I had a fine family.

3. I evidenced unshakable faith in God and lived accordingly.

You may have already defined your goals. You may have even developed a system of priorities to give order to your interests and responsibilities. I applaud such discipline and think it is useful, but I believe that this ordering process may often be a little artificial. Rarely do we fragment the life we live. It is not possible to influence one facet of life without that affecting other aspects as well. So in my own experience I have preferred not to compartmentalize my interests, but to synergize them. Let me explain what I mean.

Nephi said, "I did liken all scriptures unto us, that it might be for our profit and learning." (1 Nephi 19:23.) He was advising us to weave the fiber of scriptural wisdom into the fabric of our own being.

King Benjamin taught this interrelationship: "When ye are

29

in the service of your fellow beings, ye are only in the service of your God." (Mosiah 2:17.) As I ponder serving God, I recognize that I cannot serve him without first serving the children he has sent to bless our family. And as I ponder service to our children, I know I cannot serve them to the fullest without first serving and honoring my wife, the mother of those children. She is my highest priority. When we were married, we vowed that we would "seek . . . *first* the kingdom of God, and his righteousness." (Matthew 6:33; emphasis added.) Do you see how these goals and priorities all are indelibly intertwined? To say that your highest priority will be to your occupation or to your family or to the Lord is really much more difficult than it is to merge strengths and pursue those interests concurrently.

One of the most remarkable things about these three objectives is that they all have in common one requirement. That requirement is education. The educational process is crucial for success in each objective and is never ending.

SERVICE TO MY FELLOWMEN

First, with regard to service of worth to mankind, I am a heart surgeon—but that really doesn't tell the whole story. When I started medical school, we were taught that one must not touch the heart, for if one did, it would stop beating. But I also pondered the scripture that tells us that "all kingdoms have a law given . . . and unto every kingdom is given a law; and unto every law there are certain bounds also and conditions." (D&C 88:36, 38.) I believed sincerely the scripture that certifies that "when we obtain any blessing from God, it is by obedience to that law upon which it is predicated." (D&C 130:21.)

Knowing these scriptures while concentrating on the "kingdom" of and the blessing of the beating heart, I knew that even the function of this vital organ was predicated upon law. I reasoned that if the applicable laws could be understood and controlled, perhaps they could be utilized for the blessing of the sick. To me this meant that if we would work, study, and ask the proper questions in our scientific experiments, we could learn the laws that govern the heartbeat.

In 1949 our group of researchers presented at the American College of Surgeons the report of the first successful use of the artificial heart-lung machine in sustaining the life of an animal for thirty minutes, without its own heart powering its circulation.

In the decade of the 1950s, successes in the animal laboratory were extended to human beings. Now with many of those laws learned, the heartbeat can be turned off while delicate repairs are performed on damaged valves and vessels, and then turned on again — provided the laws are obeyed upon which that blessing is predicated. Over two hundred thousand open-heart operations are performed in the United States annually and many more worldwide, thereby extending life for many. But you should know that it was through the understanding of the scriptures, and "likening" them to this area of interest, that the great field of heart surgery as we know it today was facilitated for me.

A FINE FAMILY

Turning now from service of worth to my fellowmen, the second sentence that I hope may be said of me at my funeral would be that I had a fine family. That is really a subject near and dear to my heart, and I will not try to treat it broadly except to say that Sister Nelson has brought into our family ten beautiful children. We have tried to rear them consonant with an important scripture: "Honour thy father and thy mother: that thy days may be long upon the land which the Lord thy God giveth thee." (Exodus 20:12.)

The importance of honoring parents extends beyond one's own father and mother. This scripture implies that we honor the father and the mother of children that might yet be born to *us*. We considered this implication while dating and in the early years of our marriage. But I fully understood that concept only later when I watched Sister Nelson cradle those children

31

in her arms as they arrived one by one. Each time, she reassured herself and her newborn baby that no blessing had been withheld from that child because of any act of impurity in her life that could have deprived that infant of its full potential in any way. To honor father and mother means to honor fatherhood and motherhood and the divine provision for procreation and all that pertains to it.

Part of honoring parenthood is honoring children. There is a great temptation to believe erroneously that our children are our possessions. They are not. They are sons and daughters of our Heavenly Father. Their spirits are eternal, as are ours.

This lesson was brought forcibly to my attention many years ago when our youngest daughter was about four years of age. I came home from work one night to find my sweetheart very weary from a full day with nine children underfoot. My day had been heavy also, but I offered to get the children ready for bed. I began to give the orders to our little four-year-old daughter: take your clothes off, hang them up, brush your teeth, put on your pajamas, say your prayers, and so forth, commanding in a manner befitting a tough sergeant in the army. Suddenly she cocked her head to one side, looked at me with wistful eyes, and said, "Daddy, do you own me?"

Then I realized that I was using coercive methods on this sweet spirit, and that to rule children by command or force is the technique of Satan, not of the Savior. She taught me this important lesson. We don't own our children; we only have them for a brief season. As parents, it is our privilege to love them, to lead them, and then to let them go. The Lord said, "I have commanded you to bring up your children in light and truth." (D&C 93:40.) This we have tried to do.

Another aspect of our parental responsibility has been to be faithful to every duty we have been called to perform in the Church. Is this a paradox in priorities? No, it isn't. A scripture states: "Wherefore thy duty is unto the church forever, and this *because of* thy family." (D&C 23:3; emphasis added.) We have recognized that among the fine things we can do for our chil-

this book
Power
Hun(?)

dren is to be faithful to any Church call we have received. Experience gained in the Church strengthens our capacity to serve the public and our family.

Elder Russel M. Nelson, an apostle, and world-famous
heart surgeon
gives his testimony of education.

FAITH IN GOD

The third sentence that I hope I may merit at my funeral service is that my faith in God was unshakable. I do have a deep and abiding faith in him and in his Son, Jesus Christ.

Education has increased that faith. I have spent some forty years in the study of one of God's greatest creations, the human body, and I know that this marvelous instrument is of divine origin. The anatomy, the physiology, the protective mechanisms, the healing powers — all are well constructed and function beautifully. It is as evident to me that they are the products of a divine Creator as it must be for an astronomer to reach the same conclusion in studying the endless phenomenon of the stars in the heavens.

Furthering our education need not challenge, but should increase our faith. In fact, we have a religious responsibility to educate our minds. We have been taught that "the glory of God is intelligence." (D&C 93:36.) We have a divine command to "obtain a knowledge of history, and of countries, and of kingdoms, of laws of God and man." (D&C 93:53.) Similarly, the Lord has exhorted us to "study and learn, and become acquainted with all good books, and with languages, tongues and people." (D&C 90:15.) The scriptures further admonish, "Learn wisdom in thy youth" (Alma 37:35), and "Teach one another the doctrine of the kingdom. Teach ye diligently and my grace shall attend you" (D&C 88:77-78).

STEPS IN LEARNING

We all understand the *importance* of education. Perhaps now we should consider *how* to learn. May I suggest four steps to facilitate the learning process.

1. *Desire*. The first step in the learning process is to have a great desire to know the truth. As a teacher of surgery for

flip 2 pages

many years, I observed differences in the desires of individuals to learn. Before every operation there is an interval for scrubbing hands for a measured period of time. Some trainees were either silent or passed this time with trivial conversations that had no substance. Those with desire filled the time with questions. I observed that students with great desire knew what they didn't know and sought to fill those voids.

2. *Inquire.* The second step in the learning process is to study with an inquiring mind. Again I take this pattern from the scriptures. When the brother of Jared was preparing for a transoceanic migration, he realized that there was no provision for light in the ships, so he asked the Lord, "Shall [we] cross this great water in darkness?" The Lord gave an interesting reply: "What will ye that I should do that ye may have light in your vessels? . . . Ye cannot have windows, for they will be dashed in pieces; neither shall ye take fire with you. . . . Ye shall be as a whale in the midst of the sea." (Ether 2:22-24.)

The Lord could have told the brother of Jared. However, he left the brother of Jared to study it out in his own mind before proffering the solution. As a result, the brother of Jared selected sixteen stones and then asked the Lord to touch them so that they might provide the light.

That same concept was stressed in latter-day revelation, when the Lord told Oliver Cowdery, who wanted to help Joseph Smith translate the Book of Mormon, "You have not understood; you have supposed that I would give it unto you, when you took no thought save it was to ask me. But, behold, I say unto you, that you must study it out in your mind; then you must ask me if it be right." (D&C 9:7-8.)

Many of the revelations contained in the Doctrine and Covenants were given to prophets only after profound study and thoughtful, focused inquiry of the Lord. So it was with the Word of Wisdom, which was given through the Prophet Joseph Smith, and the revelation on the priesthood, given through President Spencer W. Kimball in 1978. Similarly, each of us will learn best with the spirit of inquiry.

3. *Apply*. The third step in the learning process is to apply or practice learning in our daily lives. Those who have learned another language know how important that is. Even with great desire and study, mastery of the language comes only as it is applied to the daily situations of life.

4. *Pray*. The fourth and very important step in the learning process is to pray for help. In my practice of surgery, I did not hesitate to communicate with the Lord in great detail, even about the technical steps in a new operative procedure that was to be performed. Often just the process of rehearsing it in my mind while engaged in prayer allowed divine direction for me to see a better way.

SAFEGUARDS TO PROTECT US

Now may I offer important words of warning. Learning, if misused, can destroy our goals. Let us consider some safeguards to protect us from such an undesirable end.

 First, our faith must be nourished. We must enrich that faith with scriptural study and with exposure to other fine books, such as books on art or music. We must nourish the gifts of the spirit on the same daily basis as we feed our physical bodies.

 Second, we must choose our role models wisely. Before we endorse the teachings or actions of any individual, we should ask ourselves if that person's *faith* is strong enough to be worthy of emulation. If it isn't, we should be very discriminating in what we learn from such an individual. The Bible, the Book of Mormon, the Doctrine and Covenants, and the Pearl of Great Price are the standards by which we should measure all doctrine.

 Third, we should avoid the mysteries and doctrinal hobby horses. God has revealed all that we need to know for our exaltation. If we will be obedient to the revealed word, we can be patient with the unrevealed. That is why we don't use the terms "orthodox" and "unorthodox" in the Church. We either believe revealed truth or we don't believe it.

35

Fourth, we should avoid poisons of faith, such as sin and pornography, or barely abiding the letter of the law instead of embracing the ennobling spirit of the law. Remember, "The letter killeth, but the spirit giveth life." (2 Corinthians 3:6.)

PREPARE FOR CHALLENGES

Many challenges have to be faced as we go through life. For example, we sometimes hear allegations that the Church is anti-intellectual. When people make such a statement, I am reminded of a common sight in the jungles of Africa. A bird, like the critic, will often perch on the uppermost part of an elephant and peck away at the hide of the stately animal, achieving temporary nourishment and a position of eminence by virtue of this association. While the elephant doesn't need the bird, the bird needs the elephant for its place of prominence. Though the bird may peck, squawk, and smear, the elephant steadily pursues its course in seeming oblivion to its parasitic passenger.

To the charge that the Church is anti-intellectual, we ourselves should be the greatest evidence to refute such an erroneous statement. Individually, we have been encouraged to learn and to seek knowledge from any dependable source. In the Church, we embrace *all* truth, whether it comes from the scientific laboratory or from the revealed word of the Lord. We accept *all* truth as being part of the gospel. One truth does not contradict another.

Some of the greatest intellectuals have been those with the strongest faith. Socrates felt that the unexamined life is not worth living, so nothing was exempt from his questioning. But he, with Immanuel Kant, had unwavering faith in God, freedom, and immortality. Socrates never doubted the will of his personal God. He believed so much in freedom that he tied his own self-responsibility to that freedom. So deeply did he believe in the doctrine of immortality of the soul that although he might have prolonged his biological life by choosing exile,

36

he submitted with complete serenity to the death sentence of the Athenean court.

Louis Pasteur made this statement on his reception into the French Academy: "The Greeks have given us one of the most beautiful words of our language, the word *enthusiasm*, which means 'a God within.' The grandeur of the acts of men is measured by the inspiration from which they spring. Happy is he who bears a God within!"

Consider the Council of the Twelve today. Almost all of them hold baccalaureate degrees, and several have earned master's and doctor's degrees. I must add that educational attainments have not qualified them for their spiritual callings, but it does indicate that their own scholarly pursuits make them not only sympathetic to, but also supportive of, the divine decrees to gain knowledge.

We all must fortify ourselves against attacks on the leaders of the Church. They have never purported to be perfect or even close to it. In fact, the Lord described them as "the weak things of the world, those who are unlearned and despised." But, he continued, they will "thrash the nations by the power of my Spirit." (D&C 35:13.)

Under brutal attack by his critics, Joseph Smith said, "I never told you I was perfect—but there is no error in the revelations which I have taught—must I then be thrown away as a thing of nought?" (*Words of Joseph Smith*, p. 369.)

As we edify ourselves with education for the eternities, we must search the scriptures, liken them unto us, learn the law in the kingdom of our own activities, and use the standard works as literal standards of eternal excellence against which we measure every thought and deed.

Let us, then, each begin with the end in mind and shape our own destiny. Remember, the development of one's career, family, and faith in God is an individual responsibility, one for which each of us, individually, will be held accountable.

Chapter 4

PROTECT THE SPIRITUAL POWER LINE

One day while trimming the hedges and vines around our home, I had an interesting experience. I was at work with my electric clippers and long extension cord. I had done this often, each time reminding myself of the need to use these clippers with great care in order to avoid cutting things that I shouldn't. Suddenly the blades became jammed. Caught between them was the power cord itself. Because I had not seen it in the thicket I was trimming, I had cut into the very line that was providing the power to work.

Isn't that one of life's great lessons? I thought. *Power, if misused, can cut into the very source of that power.*

Just as the careless use of electrical power can sever the source of that power, so it is possible to misuse spiritual power to sever our spiritual power line. We then lose that which enables us to generate success in our lives. Proper use of our spiritual power line allows us to learn, to labor, to be obedient to law, and to love. While these capabilities lead to fulfillment, at the same time they also carry risk.

Consider *the power to learn*. How essential it is for progress, whether one's career is professional or that of a salesman, a farmer, or a homemaker.

But learning can be misused! A sharp mind, misdirected, can cut into that line of spiritual power. Some "learned" souls delight in leading others astray, all in the so-called name of learning. Years later their victims may realize that they have climbed their ladder of learning, only to find it leaning against the wrong wall. A prophet of the Lord has counseled us on this point: "O that cunning plan of the evil one! O the vainness, and the frailties, and the foolishness of men! When they are learned they think they are wise, and they hearken not unto the counsel of God, for they set it aside, supposing they know of themselves, wherefore, their wisdom is foolishness and it profiteth them not. And they shall perish. But to be learned is good if they hearken unto the counsels of God." (2 Nephi 9:28-29.)

What happens without spiritual learning? What happens to the pilot of a glider when he is cut loose from the power of his tow plane? There may be banks and turns, but ultimately there is only one direction he can go, and that is down!

We must gain learning, but we must apply it wisely. Otherwise, we have politics without principle, industry without morality, knowledge without wisdom, science without humanity.

Consider *the power of labor.* Labor well spent increases our capacity to do. President Heber J. Grant often quoted Ralph Waldo Emerson, who wrote, "That which we persist in doing becomes easier for us to do; not that the nature of the thing itself is changed, but that our power to do is increased."

The Lord, through his prophet Lehi, said: "It must needs be, that there is an opposition in all things." (2 Nephi 2:11.) In reality, healthy competition forces us to improve. It deserves our praise and our gratitude. Without it we could not reach the heights that are otherwise ours to achieve.

But our labor can be misdirected. One can be anxiously engaged in a meaningless cause, or one can do something wrong a hundred times and call it experience. Some would avoid labor while pursuing the goals of wealth without working for it, or honored position without preparation for it. The converted Lamanites taught this lesson: "Rather than shed the blood of their brethren they would give up their own lives;

40

and rather than take away from a brother they would give unto him; and rather than spend their days in idleness they would labor abundantly with their hands." (Alma 24:18.)

Next, consider *the power of obedience to law.* One of the great applications of spiritual power is in obeying the laws of both God and man. *Freedom* to act and *mastery* of our actions both emanate from law. "When we obtain any blessing from God, it is by obedience to that law upon which it is predicated." (D&C 130:21.)

I relearned that so well from President Spencer W. Kimball. On one occasion when he needed an operation that I was to perform, he first asked me for a priesthood blessing. Following that, he said, "Now you may proceed to do that which must be done in order to make that blessing possible."

He knew and I knew that not even for God's prophet can anyone be exempted from law. Not even for God's Son could divine law be broken!

Consider *the power of love.* I remember a mother I met once as I made a professional house call. This woman was confined in an iron lung. The ravages of polio had effectively destroyed all the breathing muscles so that her life was completely dependent upon the large metal tank and the electrical motor that powered its noisy bellows.

While there, I watched her three children as they related to their mother. The oldest interrupted our work to ask permission to go to a friend's house for an hour. Later the second child asked her mother for help with arithmetic. Finally the youngest child, so small that she couldn't see her mother's face directly, looked up at the mother's image in a mirror that had been placed over her head and asked, "Mommy, may I have a cookie?" I've never forgotten that lesson on the power of love. This woman, virtually disabled and certainly incapable of any degree of physical enforcement of parental authority, sweetly influenced that home solely with the power to love.

The power of love between a man and a woman is special. The love shared with my beloved companion, Dantzel, has increased the power of love for both of us. That love brought us to the altar in the temple of the Lord. Her love for me motivated her to teach school during the early years of our marriage. When things were tight, she held a second job at night. Once when things were exceptionally tight, she even sold her blood in between her two jobs to keep us solvent. (Her dear parents on that occasion may have wondered what kind of a son-in-law they had!) I thought of that many years later when she needed a transfusion urgently, and her blood couldn't be matched readily with donor blood from the blood bank. What a privilege it was for me to donate my blood directly to her.

Can the power of love be misused? Sadly, yes. The illegitimate union of the sexes has, in my observation, been one of the greatest causes of grief. In some instances, the improper use of this sacred physical endowment has even destroyed its use in later years.

Misused, the power of love can cut off spiritual power. Abuse of the power of love can result in no love at all. Only its cheap facsimiles of lewdness and lust remain in the wake of pleasure without conscience. Instead of feasting at the banquet table of bounteous love with one's own posterity, one is left with scraps from the table—the refuse from what might have been.

The ashes of burned "love" smolder with the smoke of sadness; yet the embers of evil still burn. But as loud voices argue on, let us remember that those who advocate abortion have already been born. Those who freely deny God with their amoral and agnostic practices will one day find he may just as freely deny them. (See 3 Nephi 28:34.)

The source of our spiritual power is the Lord. The ultimate source of spiritual power is God our Father. The messenger of this power is the Holy Ghost. This power differs from electrical power. An electrical appliance consumes power, while the use of God's spiritual power replenishes our power. While electrical power can be used only for measured periods of time, spiritual power can be used for time and eternity.

Our spiritual power line is strengthened through prayer. As we counsel with God in all our doings, he will direct us for good. (See Alma 37:37.) Prayer is available whenever we ask for it. But the Lord places the initiative upon us. He expects us to reach for his power, just as we must insert the plug in the outlet for electricity. He said: "If thou shalt ask, thou shalt receive revelation upon revelation, knowledge upon knowledge, that thou mayest know the mysteries and peaceable things—that which bringeth joy, that which bringeth life eternal." (D&C 42:61.) Personal worthiness and scripture study enable us to do more with this power.

Rewards result from righteous use of the spiritual power belonging to the priesthood. And the rewards are so great that they are almost beyond human comprehension. To those couples who bear and share that priesthood worthily and remain faithful to the law of the everlasting covenant of eternal marriage—enduring the congested years and trials of diapers and dishes, the crowded kitchen and the thin pocketbook, service in the Church, education and the burning of the midnight oil—the Lord makes this promise: "Ye shall come forth in the first resurrection; . . . and shall inherit thrones, kingdoms, principalities, and powers, dominions, . . . [and there] shall be a fulness and a continuation of the seeds forever and ever." (D&C 132:19.)

The spiritual power line conveys revelation. Revelation is given to the prophet for the Church, and to leaders and teachers in their respective callings. Personal revelation is provided for the glorification of individual members and families. Such power lines are well insulated and they are not scrambled. Our Father is a God of order. No one else receives revelation to govern the Church; that will be delivered only to the president of the Church. A father will not receive revelation for the family of his neighbor next door.

It is possible to disregard or even misuse spiritual power.

43

Some have misused the power of prayer by making that sacred communication trivial. Some well-meaning Saints even do the right things for the wrong reasons, if they narrowly center on the percentages they report rather than the precious people they serve.

Like cutting the cord with the clippers, it is possible to use spiritual power so carelessly as to destroy one's very connection to that power. I know a husband who dominates his wife as though she were his possession. He seems to regard her about as much as he does his automobile or his suitcase, which he uses for his own purposes. And I know a wife who dominates her husband to the point that he has lost all feelings of self-worth.

Remember, "The rights of the priesthood are inseparably connected with the powers of heaven, and . . . the powers of heaven cannot be controlled nor handled only upon the principles of righteousness." (D&C 121:36.) The unrighteous use of priesthood authority surely severs the connection to the Source of that authority.

Worship strengthens the power line to Deity. There can be no true worship without sacrifice, and there can be no true sacrifice without a cause. The cause that earns our love and priority is the cause of Jesus the Christ. Speaking of his own atonement, he proclaimed, "To this end was I born, and for this cause came I into the world." (John 18:37.) His example of worship, sacrifice, and commitment to cause becomes ours. His is the ultimate source of all our power to do good. As we carefully and prayerfully protect the spiritual power line that links us to the Savior, we become more like him.

Chapter 5

OBEDIENCE AND SACRIFICE

Obedience and sacrifice are similar in that they both bring forth the blessings of heaven, but the words have quite different meanings.

SACRIFICE

The word *sacrifice* comes from two Latin roots. The first root is *sacer,* which means "sacred." This root is found in other words familiar to us, such as *sacrament*, which means "sacred thought," *consecrate*, which means "with sacredness," and, in its nasal form, the word *sanctify*. The Latin word for priest is *sacerdos*, which means "sacred doer." The Saints who speak Spanish and Portuguese will recognize the similarity to the word *sacerdocio*, which is their word for priesthood.

The second half of the word *sacrifice* comes from the Latin root *facere,* which means "to do" or "to make." We recognize this same root in such words as *factory*, a place where things are made, and *manufacture*, which means to "make by hand" (*man* meaning "hand"). This is the same root form that we see in the word *fact*, which means "deed," something that "has been done." This comes from the Latin word *factus,* which is the past participle of the verb *facere.* We see this root form in the word *benefactor*, which means "good doer."

I mention the derivation of the word *sacrifice* because it literally means "make sacred." Through common usage, the meaning of the word has been altered over the years. Thus,

45

today's dictionary defines the word to suggest that something is given up or lost.

In this context, some use the word *sacrifice*, I believe, somewhat inadvisedly to apply to "giving up" of one's gratuitous donations and service in the Church.

A quotation of President Brigham Young bears on this concept. He said, "Not one particle of all that comprises this vast creation of God is our own. Everything we have has been bestowed upon us for our action, to see what we would do with it — whether we would use it for eternal life and exaltation or for eternal death and degradation, until we cease operating in this existence. We have nothing to sacrifice: then let us not talk about sacrificing." (*Journal of Discourses* 8:67.)

The religious ordinance of sacrifice was instituted by God among men after the transgression in Eden:

> Adam and Eve . . . called upon the name of the Lord, and they heard the voice of the Lord . . . speaking unto them. . . .
>
> And he gave unto them commandments, that they should worship the Lord their God, and should offer the firstlings of their flocks, for an offering unto the Lord. . . .
>
> And after many days an angel of the Lord appeared unto Adam, saying: Why dost thou offer sacrifices unto the Lord? And Adam said unto him: I know not, save the Lord commanded me.
>
> And then the angel spake, saying: This thing is a similitude of the sacrifice of the Only Begotten of the Father, which is full of grace and truth. (Moses 5:4-7.)

It seems that every principle or ordinance of the gospel has satanic imitations. Abraham rendered this account:

> My fathers, having turned from their righteousness, and from the holy commandments which the Lord their God had given unto them, unto the worshiping of the gods of the heathen, utterly refused to hearken to my voice;
>
> For their hearts were set to do evil, and were wholly turned to the god of Elkenah. . . .
>
> Therefore they turned their hearts to the sacrifice of the heathen in offering up their children unto these dumb idols, and hearkened not unto my voice, but endeavored to take away my life by the hand of the priest of Elkenah. (Abraham 1:5-7.)

Abraham was spared by the Lord and removed from the land of the Chaldeans to accomplish the Lord's purposes. (See Abraham 1:16.)

This memory certainly became poignant many years later when the patriarch Abraham was directed by the Lord to offer his son Isaac for a sacrifice on Mount Moriah. There, the meanings of sacrifice and obedience were merged in one act. Note these excerpts from his divine decree:

> Take now thy son, thine only son Isaac....
>
> Isaac spake unto Abraham his father, and said, My father: and he said, Here am I, my son....
>
> So they went both of them together ... and [Abraham] bound Isaac his son, and laid him on the altar upon the wood.
>
> And Abraham stretched forth his hand, and took the knife to ... his son.
>
> And the angel of the Lord called unto him out of heaven, and said, Abraham, Abraham: ...
>
> Lay not thine hand upon the lad, neither do thou any thing unto him: for now I know that thou fearest God, seeing thou hast not withheld thy son, thine only son from me....
>
> [A ram was offered] in the stead of his son.
>
> Thou ... hast not withheld thy son, thine only son. (Genesis 22:2, 7-13, 16.)

As this story is recorded, the word *son* is used repeatedly. It is easy to comprehend the teaching of Jacob that this action of Abraham and Isaac was "a similitude of God and his Only Begotten Son." (Jacob 4:5.) As we honor Abraham, we honor Isaac as well, for Jewish tradition holds that Isaac was no child, but a mature man who also knowingly and willingly obeyed. If so, this component of the similitude further typified the willingness and obedience that characterized the atoning sacrifice of the Savior of the world. The simile continues in that the journey from Mount Moriah back to their home in Beersheba, where life could be taken up again, took Abraham and Isaac three days, the same interval as that between the sacrifice of the Savior and his return to life as the resurrected Lord.

From the days of Adam to the time when the atonement

47

was consummated, sacrifice by the shedding of blood was instituted by God among men. In addition to similitude of the eventual atonement, it taught them the reality that mortal life is dependent upon blood. The atoning sacrifice involved the shedding of blood, both in Gethsemane and on Calvary. This was required in order that the resurrected body might again live in the same bloodless condition as it was with Adam in its paradisiacal state prior to the fall.

The sacrificial rites involving the shedding of blood, which had been practiced from the time of Adam, were to prepare the world and its people for the supreme sacrifice of the Lamb of God. Thus, the atonement of the Lord fulfilled the law of Moses, which included blood sacrifice. "We are sanctified through the offering of the body of Jesus Christ once for all. . . . For by one offering he hath perfected for ever them that are sanctified." (Hebrews 10:10, 14.)

No longer do we think in terms of shedding blood or sacrificing animals. Rarely should we focus in terms of "giving up" time and means. Instead, we should now revert to the original meaning of the word — that we "make sacred." For us to sacrifice, we should "make sacred" every thought, every action, and our very character.

King David perceived the need for personal commitment in sacrifice when he said: "Neither will I offer . . . offerings unto the Lord my God of that which doth cost me nothing." (2 Samuel 24:24.) The giving of our time and means should not be the end in itself, but a means to the end of making ourselves sacred. Each, by living a saintly life, can present to the Lord one more sanctified soul to the honor and glory of his Creator.

OBEDIENCE

Next let us examine the word *obedience*, which means "to obey." The word *obey* has an interesting derivation. It also comes from two Latin roots. The prefix *ob* means "to" or "toward." The second half of the word is a form of the Latin word *audire*, which means "to hear" or "to listen." This root occurs in such words as *audience, auditorium, audio* — all pertaining to the process of listening. Literally, then, the word *obey* means "listen to."

Searching through the scriptures listed under the topic of obedience in the Topical Guide, I found that the majority of Old Testament citations stem from the Hebrew word *shama,* meaning "to hear intelligently." It applies to hearing the voice of God and being obedient to his word. The majority of the scriptures listed for the New Testament, however, do not carry that same application. (Wives obey husbands, children obey parents, servants obey masters, and so forth.) Interestingly, the citations from the Book of Mormon, largely from writings of the time of the Old Testament, predominantly carry the same emphasis on the earlier application: hearing or listening to the authoritative word of God and being obedient to it.

One cannot be obedient unless there is authoritative word to be heard. Speaking in a gospel context, that means there cannot be obedience without there first being knowledge of the word of God. Moreover, one cannot be obedient (or disobedient) to that word without exercising the divine gift of agency. Individuals are free to choose to obey the word of God or to disobey it. Their choice becomes their response, and it has moral value. Coercion has no place in the kingdom of God because it does not elicit moral action and is therefore contrary to his gift of agency.

Agency is not entirely free, nor is it a self-preserving gift. It must be earned and it must be protected. In choosing one's career, for example, one may select any occupation one wishes in order to earn the right to act freely in that occupation. I am not free to be a concert pianist because I have not earned that right. (I forfeited that option at age ten, much to the dismay of my mother.) For many years I did the work of a surgeon because I had earned the requisite knowledge and certification on which that freedom was based. Then, interestingly, with a few brief words from the prophets of God that I was to be sustained as a member of the Quorum of the Twelve, I was

49

free to give up the earned choice to be a surgeon, and to exercise my agency to obey the new call. Each of us is free to be obedient, and that choice each freely and consciously makes as an individual.

Each of us has not only been tested in the past, but will also face trials in the future. If a call comes to leave the comfort and convenience of present surroundings to serve elsewhere, will that call be greeted with the question, "When?" Eventually, two prophets will be called to Jerusalem, where they will be slain in streets sanctified not only by their service, but also by the service of their Savior. (See Revelation 1:14; D&C 77:15; Zechariah 4:11-14.) Our choice to serve must be an informed choice based on eternal truths, for we do not obey blindly, but because we can see. We faithfully follow God's eternal plan and honor our sacred role in it.

President Stephen L Richards said: "There are some, perhaps who may feel that it is subversive of individual freedom of thought and expression to be controlled by the interpretations of our leaders. I wish to assure them that any feeling of constraint will disappear when once they secure the genius and true spirit of this work. Our unanimity of thought and action does not arise, as some suppose, from duress or compulsion in any form. Our accord comes from universal agreement with righteous principles and common response to the operation of the Spirit of our Father. It is actuated by no fear except one. That is the fear of offending God, the Author of our work." (*Conference Report*, October 1938, p. 116.)

The word to be heard from divine authority is that Joseph Smith saw and heard God the Father and his Son Jesus Christ, that he received revelations for the Church, and that he translated the Book of Mormon from engraved plates delivered to him by a heavenly being. All the doctrines that have emanated from these divine manifestations are those of the Church. One cannot accept some and reject others.

The destiny of Zion therefore depends on true education — not the education of worldly wisdom, but the education that has for its basis the incontrovertible truths of the knowledge of God and the glorious principles revealed by him in these latter days. Nothing in this world is of so much importance to us as obedience to the gospel of Jesus Christ. Inactivity may involve disobedience, but obedience must be preceded by faith as well as knowledge. "Whoso treasureth up my word, shall not be deceived." (JS–Matthew 1:37.)

May I review a few pages of medical history to show what a high price has been paid for scriptural illiteracy. I will first cite a few highlights of that history and then follow with relevant scriptural quotations.

Through nearly all but the most recent periods of recorded medical literature, the dogma had prevailed that infections were spread from one individual to another by means of air pollution. One of the earliest publications bears a dateline of 1690, when Robert Boyle of London wrote his "Experimental Discourse on Some Unheeded Causes of the Insalubrity and Salubrity of the Air." In 1772 John Evelyn reported his work entitled "Aer, and Smoake of London," noting that "thousands of infants suffocated every year by smoake and stenches which good policy might in great measure remove." Tenon reported in 1788 that in the Hôtel-Dieu in Paris, three to six patients occupied one bed. Surgical cases and women after childbirth were distributed three and four in the same bed.

Even in one of the major hospitals in the United States of America as recently as 1932, more than one patient occupied a bed at the same time. Yet, even by such an authority as Lord Lister (1867), air pollution was still blamed for infections! And in 1869 Simpson from Edinburgh and in 1875 Stimson from New York independently urged that hospitals be taken down and rebuilt every year or two.

Meanwhile, as Brigham Young and the pioneers were entering Salt Lake Valley in 1847, the Austrian physician Semmelweiss advanced the new idea that childbirth fever could be prevented by cleansing hands and linens. His report was greeted with furious debate and disbelief. Thanks to the work

51

of Pasteur, Koch, and others, within the last century this concept changed. They demonstrated that disease can be transmitted directly from one infected person to another, and they proved that germs, and not air, were the means by which infections were spread.

Now, with this brief panorama of man's scientific struggle in your mind, may I invite your attention to the word of the Lord given to all mankind, even centuries before the time of Christ. As you read this, imagine a person with drainage from any infected wound:

> And the Lord spake unto Moses and to Aaron, saying,
> Speak unto the children of Israel, and say unto them, When any man hath a running issue [drainage] out of his flesh, *because of his issue* he is unclean.
> And this shall be his uncleanness in his issue: whether his flesh run with his issue, or his flesh be stopped from his issue, it is his uncleanness.
> Every bed, whereon he lieth that hath the issue, is unclean: and every thing, whereon he sitteth, shall be unclean.
> And whosoever toucheth his bed shall wash his clothes, and bathe himself in water, and be unclean until the even.
> And he that sitteth on any thing whereon he sat that hath the issue shall wash his clothes, and bathe himself in water, and be unclean until the even.
> And he that toucheth the flesh of him that hath the issue shall wash his clothes, and bathe himself in water, and be unclean until the even. . . .
> And when he that hath an issue is cleansed of his issue; then he shall number to himself seven days for his cleansing, and wash his clothes, and bathe his flesh in running water, and shall be clean. (Leviticus 15:1-7, 13; emphasis added.)

Thus, in the scriptures the Lord clearly revealed in detail the procedures and importance of clean technique in the handling of infected patients.

In 1970 the United States Public Health Service published a monograph entitled "Isolation Techniques for Use in Hospitals," which is the standard for current hospital practice. The principles given in this document are the same as those cited from Leviticus. Further, on page 9 we read the following:

"Handwashing before and after contact with each patient is the single most important means of preventing the spread of infection"—essentially the same message as that recorded in Leviticus over three thousand years ago!

How many mothers have needlessly perished? How many children have suffered because mankind's studies failed to include the knowledge of or obedience to the word of God? Whether one examines the annals of medicine or any other record of human life on this earth, the message is always the same: Know and obey the commandments, and you will earn the blessings of God; fail to obey the commandments, and grief necessarily follows.

How glorious will be the day when the enlightening message of our missionaries may be taken to the underprivileged nations of the earth so that the word of God can be heard and obeyed. Their people will be blessed by the prosperity that obedience will bring.

In our efforts to proclaim the virtue of obedience, we might unwisely teach with inappropriate emphasis. For example, many important facts and figures are sometimes cited to illustrate the great physical benefits that come from obedience to the Word of Wisdom. We know that cigarette smoking is the single most important preventable cause of heart disease, cancer, artery disease, and lung disease. But do we obey the Word of Wisdom because medical science affirms the physical benefits that follow?

To test that concept, what would be your response if, as a parent, you were told that your son should be obedient to the Word of Wisdom even if medical science had evidence (which it does not) to suggest that such obedience would be harmful to his health? What would you do? Would you follow the counsel of medical science, or would you listen to and follow the word of God?

What did Abraham do? There was nothing to suggest that the action God had directed for him would be beneficial to

Isaac's health. Quite the contrary. Both Abraham and Isaac knew otherwise.

Or take another example. When the Israelites were being led by Joshua into the promised land, they were instructed to traverse the river Jordan. This meant 600,000 Israelite warriors and their families must be moved across a river so full that it was overflowing its banks. Their caravan was led by priests carrying the ark of the Lord. It was only when the soles of the feet of the faithful Israelites actually rested in the water that the waters were suddenly stopped and "heaped up" to allow them to cross an empty river bed. (See Joshua 3.) There was nothing to suggest that their obedience was to be beneficial to their physical health. They obeyed because of their faith in the word of God, and they were his people!

If we should focus on the physical, to the exclusion of the spiritual, benefits of obedience to the Word of Wisdom, then our sons and daughters could easily rationalize that "just one cigarette won't hurt" or "just one drink won't matter."

This is not the question. The question is one of faith. Either one has the faith to hear and obey the word of God and accept it as such, or one does not. "Without faith it is impossible to please him." (Hebrews 11:6.) Note these words of Mormon: "Wo be unto him that will not hearken unto the words of Jesus, and also to them whom he hath chosen and sent among them; for whoso receiveth not the words of Jesus and the words of those whom he hath sent receiveth not him; and therefore he will not receive them at the last day; and it would be better for them if they had not been born." (3 Nephi 28:34-35.)

Many have difficulty accepting the word of God because it comes from their contemporaries — their neighborhood bishops and local leaders who seem to be just ordinary men. Even the prophets of God are just ordinary men, but with extraordinary callings to communicate divine doctrine. We must have the faith to know that "his word [we] shall receive, as if from [his] own mouth, in all patience and faith." (D&C 21:5.) "Surely the Lord God will do nothing, but he revealeth his secret unto his servants the prophets." (Amos 3:7.)

It is particularly challenging to respond when the word of the Lord comes from one as close as one's father. I am inspired by the faith of Nephi. Lehi's family had traveled the hot desert sands of Palestine from Jerusalem to reach the eastern shore of the Red Sea, a distance that could have been as great as 250 miles. Then Lehi told his sons, Nephi and his brothers, that they must return to Jerusalem to obtain the plates of brass held by Laban. No wonder those brothers murmured when they contemplated more arduous and difficult travel under such hot and humid circumstances. It was in that setting that these words of faithful Nephi were uttered: "I will go and do the things which the Lord hath commanded, for I know that the Lord giveth no commandments unto the children of men, save he shall prepare a way for them that they may accomplish the thing which he commandeth them." (1 Nephi 3:7.)

After the young men successfully accomplished this mission, they returned to their parents only to have Lehi give them the word of the Lord that they must return to Jerusalem again. Even their mother, Sariah, murmured on that occasion.

The challenge of obedience to the word of a contemporary prophet is not new. The Lord commanded Saul, through the prophet Samuel, to "smite Amulek, and utterly destroy all that [the Amalekites] have." Saul chose to rationalize. He spared Agag and the best of the sheep and other animals and the best of all that was good, and selectively destroyed only that which was vile and refuse. Then he deceitfully reported to Samuel that he had performed the commandment of the Lord.

Samuel said, "What meaneth then this bleating of the sheep in mine ears, and the lowing of the oxen which I hear?" Saul indicated that he had spared these choice animals in order that they could be sacrificed unto the Lord. Then Samuel thundered that eternal truth: "Behold, to obey is better than sacrifice, and to hearken than the fat of rams. For rebellion is as

THE POWER WITHIN US

the sin of witchcraft, and stubbornness is as iniquity and idol-atry." (See 1 Samuel 15:1-23.)

The people in Samuel's time, like the people in our day, desired to be like their neighbors. When Samuel was the prophet, they pled with him to give them a king. Although Samuel, obedient to the counsel of the Lord, cautioned them against having a king, the people rejected this counsel. "And the Lord said unto Samuel, Hearken unto the voice of the people in all that they say unto thee: for they have not rejected thee, but they have rejected me." (1 Samuel 8:7.)

When we rationalize, reject, or rebel against the word of the prophets, we do it unto God. It is possible to discipline one's life to receive any blessing one is willing to earn. But those blessings may not come immediately, and they may inure to the benefit of others, even generations not seen.

The noble sacrifices of each nation's patriots have been a necessary prerequisite in order that the blessings of the gospel may be enjoyed in freedom by those who would come later.

The suffering and sacrifice of pioneers who built temples with a trowel in one hand and a rifle in the other enabled the blessings of the endowment to be conferred upon countless numbers who had died before and who would yet be born, long after the life of those laboring hands had passed from this mortal sphere.

The obedience and sacrifice of the Prophet Joseph Smith required his ministry to sanctify the cells of unworthy and unwarranted jails. On one of those occasions, just five years before his martyrdom, the Lord consoled the Prophet:

> If thou art called to pass through tribulation; if thou art in perils among false brethren; if thou art in perils among robbers; if thou art in perils by land or by sea;
>
> If thou art accused with all manner of false accusations; if thine enemies fall upon thee; if they tear thee from the society of thy father and mother and brethren and sisters; and if with a drawn sword thine enemies tear thee from the bosom of thy wife, and of thine offspring, and thine elder son, although but six years of age, shall cling to thy garments, and shall say, My father, my father, why can't you stay with us? ...

And above all, if the very jaws of hell shall gape open the mouth wide after thee, know thou, my son, that all these things shall give thee experience, and shall be for thy good. (D&C 122:5-7.)

Then the Lord reminded Joseph: "The Son of Man hath descended below them all. . . . Fear not what man can do, for God shall be with you forever and ever." (D&C 122:8-9.) That timeless perspective was precious to the Prophet.

The third Article of Faith states: "We believe that through the Atonement of Christ, all mankind may be saved, by obedience to the laws and ordinances of the Gospel." Christ's atoning act transcends the concept of time, affecting limitless numbers of souls for all eternity. It does so because of his choice and his preparation to be obedient to divine law.

Not even for God's Son could divine law be broken. This plaintive plea was spoken at the time of his atonement: "And he said, Abba, Father, all things are possible unto thee; take away this cup from me: nevertheless not what I will, but what thou wilt." (Mark 14:36.) Later he cried out, "Eloi, Eloi, lama sabachthani? which is, being interpreted, My God, my God, why hast thou forsaken me?" (Mark 15:34.)

Through the love that he bore for his Son, God let the full weight of the atonement bear down on the Savior, that the victory over death might be his and his alone.

Eliza R. Snow caught the significance of this in these words that we often sing:

How great the wisdom and the love
That filled the courts on high
And sent the Savior from above
To suffer, bleed, and die!

By strict obedience Jesus won
The prize with glory rife:
"Thy will, O God, not mine be done,"
Adorned his mortal life.
(Hymns, no. 195.)

Christ's example of obedience and sacrifice becomes ours.

How grateful we should be for the word of God and that we can choose to hear it and obey. We are privileged to offer sacrifice by making sacred the thoughts and deeds of our lives so that they might be more like his. In so doing, the blessings of heaven may be ours now and forever.

Chapter 6

SELF-MASTERY

I should like to discuss our quest for self-mastery. In so doing, I would converse as a loving father counseling one of my own children.

Before you can master yourself, my precious one, you need to know who you are. You consist of two parts—your physical body and your spirit, which lives within your body. You may have heard the expression "mind over matter." That's what I would like to talk about—but phrase it a little differently: "spirit over body." That is self-mastery.

When you arrived as a newborn baby, your little body was master. You had what I call the "I want what I want when I want it" philosophy. No amount of discussion could postpone your impatient demands when you wanted to be fed—and now!

Like all parents, we anxiously anticipated the first smile, a word, a glimpse at the potential of the spirit within your tiny body. Is there a mother who has not cradled her baby as your sweet mother did, in wistful wonder of the destiny of her dear little one?

Through those early years, we parents are properly concerned with physical needs of our children, such as food, clothing, and shelter. But as you grow older, our concerns shift more toward your spiritual growth, in order that you might achieve your full potential. "For the natural man is an enemy to God, and has been from the fall of Adam, and will be, forever

59

and ever, unless he yields to the enticings of the Holy Spirit . . . and becometh a saint." (Mosiah 3:19.)

That requires self-mastery. Remember, "The spirit and the body are the soul of man." (D&C 88:15.) Both are of great importance. Your physical body is a magnificent creation of God. It is his temple as well as yours, and it must be treated with reverence. Scripture declares: "Ye are the temple of God. . . . If any man defile [it], him shall God destroy; for the temple of God is holy, which temple ye are." (1 Corinthians 3:16-17.)

Remarkable as your body is, its prime purpose is of even greater importance — to serve as tenement for your spirit. Abraham taught that our spirits existed before and shall have no end, for they are eternal. (See Abraham 3:18.)

Your spirit acquired a body at birth and became a soul to live in mortality through periods of trial and testing. Part of each test is to determine if your body can become mastered by the spirit that dwells within it.

Although your spirit had a veil of forgetfulness placed over it at the time of your birth into mortality, it retained its power to remember all that happens — precisely recording each event of life. Indeed, scriptures warn that "every idle word that men shall speak, they shall give account thereof in the day of judgment." (Matthew 12:36.) Prophets refer to our "bright recollection" (Alma 11:43) and "perfect remembrance" (Alma 5:18) at that day of decision.

Since thoughts precede deeds, you must first learn to control your thoughts. "As [a man] thinketh in his heart, so is he." (Proverbs 23:7.)

In your quest for self-mastery, full participation in the activities of the Church will help. I'll mention but a few.

A first step comes as we learn together to keep the Sabbath day holy. This is one of the Ten Commandments. (See Exodus 20:8; Deuteronomy 5:15.) We honor the Sabbath "to pay [our] devotions unto the Most High" (D&C 59:10) and because the Lord declared: "It is a sign between me and you throughout your generations; that ye may know that I am the Lord that doth sanctify you" (Exodus 31:13; see also Ezekiel 20:20).

Another step toward self-mastery comes when you are old enough to observe the law of the fast. As funds are contributed from meals missed, the needs of the poor may be met. Meanwhile, through your spirit, you develop personal power over your body's drives of hunger and thirst. Fasting gives you confidence to know that your spirit can master appetite.

Some time ago your mother and I visited a third-world country where sanitary conditions were much poorer than ours. We joined with a delegation of other doctors from all over the world. The president of our group, an experienced traveler, warned of risks. In order to avoid water that might be contaminated, we were even counseled to brush our teeth with an alcoholic beverage. We chose not to follow that counsel, but simply did what we had learned to do once a month. We fasted that first day, thinking we could introduce simple food and fluids gradually thereafter. Later, we were the only ones in our group without disabling illness.

Fasting fortifies discipline over appetite and helps to protect against later uncontrolled cravings and gnawing habits.

Another step toward self-mastery comes from obedience to the Word of Wisdom. Remember, it contains a "promise, adapted to the capacity of ... the weakest of all saints." (D&C 89:3.) It was given "in consequence of evils and designs which do and will exist in the hearts of conspiring men in the last days." (D&C 89:4.) Indeed, as you develop courage to say no to alcohol, tobacco, and stimulants, you gain additional strength. You can then refuse conspiring men — those seditious solicitors of harmful substances or smut. You can reject their evil enticements to your body.

If you yield to anything that can addict, and thus defy the Word of Wisdom, your spirit surrenders to the body. The flesh then enslaves the spirit. This is contrary to the purpose of your mortal existence. And in the process of such addiction, your life span is likely to be shortened, thereby reducing the time

61

available for repentance by which your spirit might attain self-mastery over your body.

Other physical appeals come during your courtship period. In your youth, you may be challenged by restraints of parents hoping to guide you through this wonderful period of life. Because the adversary is keenly aware of the power of physical temptation, Alma instructed his son and all of us: "See that ye bridle all your passions." (Alma 38:12.) When you marry, you and your eternal companion may then invoke the power of procreation, that you may have joy and rejoicing in your posterity. This divine endowment is guarded by your Creator's law of chastity. All through the years, remember: chastity is the powerful protector of virile manhood and the crown of beautiful womanhood.

In courtship and marriage, virtue seems to come under attack first. Mental turmoil that trails in the wake of weakness from lust has evoked many a tear from innocent loved ones. Without repentance, tumult within self does not quit either. Shakespeare expressed such self-conflict as one of his characters contemplating conquest in lust spoke these lines:

> What win I, if I gain the thing I seek?
> A dream, a breath, a froth of fleeting joy.
> Who buys a minute's mirth to wail a week?
> Or sells eternity to get a toy?
> For one sweet grape who will the vine destroy?
> ("Lucrece," lines 211-15.)

Prophets have repeatedly cautioned about moral sin. One, for example, warned: "O, my beloved brethren, remember the awfulness in transgressing against that Holy God, and also the awfulness of yielding to the enticings of that cunning one. Remember, to be carnally-minded is death, and to be spiritually-minded is life eternal." (2 Nephi 9:39.)

Now don't misunderstand me. I would not want you to neglect your body. It deserves daily care. Physical conditioning through regular exercise requires self-mastery too. I marvel at Elder Joseph Anderson, now (1985) in his ninety-sixth year.

For decades, the strength of his spirit over his body has induced him to swim regularly. But his motivation has never been to attain physical longevity. That has come only incidentally. His desire has been to serve God and His anointed. Elder Anderson has followed what I label as the Lord's prescription for a long and useful life. Those faithful in "magnifying their calling, are sanctified by the Spirit unto the renewing of their bodies. They become . . . the elect of God." (D&C 84:33-34.)

Elder Anderson's philosophy of exercise agrees with the perspective of Paul, who said: "Bodily exercise profiteth little: but godliness is profitable unto all things, having promise of the life that now is, and of that which is to come." (1 Timothy 4:8.) Handsome and fit, Elder Anderson personifies this scripture: "Glorify God in your body, and in your spirit, which are God's." (1 Corinthians 6:20.)

As you work during the productive years of life, whether at home or in the field, in the factory or at a workbench, remember that reputation is built and character is forged as you develop self-mastery. Faithful payment of tithing is part of that process. It defends you against dishonesty or shabby temptations. Courageous accountability for your own actions becomes a cherished prize.

It really matters what you listen to, what you look at, what you think, say, and do. Select music that will strengthen your spirit. Control your speech; keep it free from profanity and vulgarity. Follow the teachings of this proverb: "My mouth shall speak truth; and wickedness is an abomination to my lips. All the words of my mouth are in righteousness; there is nothing . . . perverse in them." (Proverbs 8:7-8.)

As you approach old age, you will face new challenges to self-mastery. Symptoms of the deteriorating body can be painful, even disabling. Deep aches of sadness are caused by the departing of loved ones. For some, these deepening trials come early in life. But when yours are thrust upon you, remember a concept expressed by my father some time after my mother had passed away. Your grandparents had been married for sixty-four years. When someone asked how he was doing, my father simply stated, "I'm lonely, but I'm not lonesome." Do you know what he meant? Though he was now without his sweetheart, he was so busy assisting family and friends that he had replaced sorrow with service and had displaced self-pity with selfless love. He had found joy in following the timeless example of the Master.

Jesus, our Savior, was born in the lowliest of circumstances. For his baptism he was immersed in the lowest body of fresh water upon the planet. In service and suffering, he also "descended below" all things (see D&C 122:8), so that he could rise above all things. Near the end of his life, he triumphantly declared, "I have overcome the world." (John 16:33.) "Look unto me, and endure to the end, and ye shall live; for unto him that endureth to the end will I give eternal life." (3 Nephi 15:9.)

Scriptures tutor us to endure to the end to attain eternal life. Then we will obtain a resurrected body—one that is incorruptible, glorified, and prepared to live in the presence of God.

To reach your highest destiny, emulate the Savior. He proclaimed, "What manner of men ought ye to be?...Even as I am." (3 Nephi 27:27.) Our loftiest hope is to grow in spirit and attain "the stature of the fulness of Christ: that we henceforth be no more children." (Ephesians 4:13-14.)

You will then be well prepared for that pending day of judgment when, as taught by President Spencer W. Kimball, "The soul, composed of the resurrected body and the eternal spirit,...will come before the great judge to receive its final assignment for the eternity." (*The Teachings of Spencer W. Kimball*, p. 46.)

Remember, my dear one, not an age in life passes without temptation, trial, or torment experienced through your physical body. But as you prayerfully develop self-mastery, desires of the flesh may be subdued. And when that has been achieved, you may have the strength to submit to your Heavenly Father, as did Jesus, who said, "Not my will, but thine, be done." (Luke 22:42.)

When deepening trials come your way, remember this glorious promise of the Savior: "To him that overcometh will I grant to sit with me in my throne, even as I also overcame, and am set down with my Father in his throne." (Revelation 3:21.)

Christ is our great Exemplar. I declare, as a special witness, that he is the Son of God and "is the life and the light of the world." (Alma 38:9.) We develop self-mastery as we become more like him.

Chapter 7

IN THE LORD'S
OWN WAY

Because my medical work took us to a number of developing nations, Sister Nelson and I have been exposed to many challenging scenes. In one country, so many people were sleeping in the streets and on sidewalks that we literally had to step over them as we walked. In another nation, our compassion was stretched almost to the breaking point as we yearned to help countless people in need. Young mothers with babies bundled on their backs begged for money while paddling their little sampan boats, which served as both their shelter and their mode of transportation. And oh, how our hearts ached for young men and women of another country who were strapped as beasts of burden to wooden-wheeled carts laden with weighty cargo. As far as our eyes could see, the endless caravan of vehicles continued, pulled by dint of human toil.

Although reasons vary according to time and place, the poor and the needy have nearly always been present. Regardless of cause, our Heavenly Father is concerned about them. They are all his children. He loves and cares for them.

In the Old Testament we learn that when the Lord sent prophets to call Israel back from apostasy, in almost every instance one of the first charges made was that the poor had been neglected. The scriptures teach that the poor, especially widows, orphans, and strangers, have long been the concern of God and the godly. The poor have been specially favored

67

by the law. In Old Testament times, poor persons at harvest time were allowed to glean after the reapers. At fruit-picking time, what was left hanging on branches belonged to the poor. In the sabbatical seventh year and in the jubilee fiftieth year, land was not planted nor tilled, and what grew of itself was free for the hungry.

Blessings were also promised to those who cared for the poor. The Lord would deliver them in time of trouble. (See Psalm 41:1.) Truths were taught by these proverbs: "He that hath mercy on the poor, happy is he" (Proverbs 14:21), and "The righteous considereth the cause of the poor: but the wicked regardeth not to know it" (Proverbs 29:7).

During the Savior's earthly ministry, he reemphasized his timeless concern for the poor. Remember the reply he gave to the question of the rich man: "If thou wilt be perfect," he said, "go and sell [all] that thou hast, and give to the poor, and thou shalt have treasure in heaven: and come and follow me." (Matthew 19:21; see also Luke 18:22.)

In one of his precious parables, the Master illustrated this doctrine with the story of one who was hungry and was given meat, another who was thirsty and was given drink, and a stranger who was welcomed. The Lord related those as favors to him when he taught, "Verily I say unto you, Inasmuch as ye have done it unto one of the least of these my brethren, ye have done it unto me." And when they were *not* ministered unto, he admonished: "Verily I say unto you, Inasmuch as ye did it *not* to one of the least of these, ye did it *not* to me." (Matthew 25:40, 45; emphasis added.)

Indeed, the Church in New Testament times had a binding obligation to care for the poor!

The Book of Mormon repeatedly declares this doctrine. From it we learn that care of the poor is an obligation that we take upon ourselves at the time of baptism. The prophet Alma taught: "Ye are desirous to come into the fold of God, and to be called his people, and are willing to bear one another's burdens, that they may be light; yea, and [ye] are willing to mourn with those that mourn; yea, and comfort those that stand in need of comfort, and to stand as witnesses of God at all times and in all things ... even until death. ... Serve him and keep his commandments." (Mosiah 18:8-10.)

Every person who is baptized and who receives the gift of the Holy Ghost, which seals the ordinance, is under solemn covenant with the Lord to obey his commandments. Caring for the poor is one of those commandments. Surely, in Book of Mormon times, members of the Church had a sacred obligation to care for the poor.

Few, if any, of the Lord's instructions are stated more often or given greater emphasis than the commandment to care for the poor and the needy. Our dispensation is no exception. In December 1830, the very year in which the Church was organized, the Lord decreed that "the poor and the meek shall have the gospel preached unto them, and they shall be looking forth for the time of my coming, for it is nigh at hand." (D&C 35:15.)

Bishops were designated and their duties defined: "They shall look to the poor and the needy, and administer to their relief that they shall not suffer." (D&C 38:35.)

In 1831, the Lord said: "Remember the poor. ... And inasmuch as ye impart of your substance unto the poor, ye will do it unto me." (D&C 42:30-31.) A little later, he again declared, "Visit the poor and the needy and administer to their relief." (D&C 44:6.) Later the same year he warned: "Wo unto you rich men, that will not give your substance to the poor, for your riches will canker your souls." (D&C 56:16.)

With these teachings throbbing in our minds, stated and restated in accounts to all people in all days of recorded scripture, let our thoughts return to the homeless, beggars in boats, human beasts of burden, and multitudes stricken with poverty.

Is it possible to be faithful to our solemn obligation to care for the poor and needy, to lift them and to love them — worldwide? Where shall we begin? When? How? Hear the answer of Almighty God:

> I, the Lord, stretched out the heavens, and built the earth, my very handiwork; and all things therein are mine.
>
> And it is my purpose to provide for my saints, for all things are mine.
>
> But it must needs be done in mine own way; and behold this is the way that I, the Lord, have decreed to provide for my saints, that the poor shall be exalted, in that the rich are made low.
>
> For the earth is full, and there is enough and to spare; yea, I prepared all things, and have given unto the children of men to be agents unto themselves.
>
> Therefore, if any man shall take of the abundance which I have made, and impart not his portion, according to the law of my gospel, unto the poor and the needy, he shall, with the wicked, lift up his eyes in hell, being in torment. (D&C 104:14-18.)

I repeat the Lord's prescription: "But it must needs be done *in mine own way*." (D&C 104:16; emphasis added.) We begin where we are now, and work according to his plan. His "own way" includes these principles: "Women have claim on their husbands for their maintenance.... All children have claim upon their parents ... and after that, they have claim upon the church, or ... upon the Lord's storehouse, if their parents have not.... And the storehouse shall be kept by the consecrations of the church; and widows and orphans shall be provided for, as also the poor." (D&C 83:2, 4-6.)

An important part of the Lord's storehouse is maintained as a year's supply is stored, where possible, in the homes of faithful families of the Church.

Some may ask, "What about those who are poor because they are idle and unwilling to work?" Such individuals should heed these words of warning: "Thou shalt not be idle; for he that is idle shall not eat the bread nor wear the garments of the laborer." (D&C 42:42.) "Wo unto you poor men ... who will not labor with your own hands." (D&C 56:17.)

Judgment of worthiness is made by the bishop—and ultimately by the Lord, as taught by Nephi: "With righteousness shall the Lord God judge the poor, and reprove with equity for the meek of the earth." (2 Nephi 30:9.) Ours is not to judge, but ours is a covenantal obligation to care for the poor and the needy and to prepare for their rejoicing when the Messiah shall come again. (See D&C 56:18-19.)

The Lord's "own way" includes reliance first on self and then on the family. As parents care for children, the children in turn may reciprocate when parents become less able. Family pride promotes solicitude for each member, taking priority over other assistance.

If family members can't help, the Lord's "own way" includes the Church organization. The bishop is assisted by priesthood quorums and sisters of the Relief Society, organized to look "to the wants of the poor, searching after objects of charity, and administering to their wants." (*Handbook of the Relief Society,* 1931, pp. 21-22.)

Members of priesthood quorums and groups have a duty to rehabilitate, spiritually and temporally, their erring or unfortunate brethren. While a bishop extends aid to a person temporarily out of work, the quorum arranges for employment until the individual is fully self-supporting again.

As members of the Church, you and I each participate in the Lord's "own way." At least once a month, we may fast and pray and contribute generous offerings to funds that enable bishops to disburse aid. This is part of the law of the gospel. Each of us can truly help the poor and the needy—now, and wherever they are. And we too will be blessed and protected from apostasy by so doing.

Limitations do exist. Measures of relief are at best temporary. Storehouses can provide only for some temporal needs. People cannot all be brought to the same living standards. And not all needed things can be achieved by goods or gold.

To care fully for the poor, the poor must change. As they are taught and abide doctrines of Deity, spiritual strength will come that enlightens the mind and liberates the soul from the yoke of bondage. When people of the earth accept the gospel of Christ, their attitudes change and their understanding and capabilities increase.

71

A poet sensed the great power of the Spirit of the Lord to lift an individual when he wrote:

> The chief of all thy wondrous work,
> Supreme of all thy plan,
> Thou hast put an upward reach
> Within the heart of man.

That upward reach, drawn from a knowledge of divine doctrines, transforms souls. May I share an illustration with you.

Some time ago Sister Nelson and I were invited to the humble home of Polynesian Saints who had relatively recently joined the Church. By walking carefully on wooden planks, we approached their house, built on wooden piles emerging from the floor of the sea, and climbed a ladder to enter their little one-room dwelling. As we sat on freshly woven grass mats, we could peek through holes in the floor and view sea water below. That home was starkly devoid of furniture except for a used sewing machine provided by sisters of the Relief Society. But the love and warmth of this special family were apparent.

"We would like to sing for you," the father said through an interpreter. He put one arm around his wife and the other around the children, as did his wife. Five little ones, dressed in newly sewn clothing, joined their parents in singing songs the father had composed. At the conclusion, he said, "These songs express our feelings of deep gratitude. Before we joined the Church, we had so little. Now we have so much! Our lives have been greatly blessed by membership in the Church."

As we wiped tears from our moistened cheeks, Sister Nelson and I looked at each other, comprehending that the gospel brings spiritual wealth that may bear little relation, at first, to tangible abundance. Conversely, people with plenty can be spiritually poor. Yet the Lord is concerned for them all.

Missionary work throughout the world is part of the Lord's plan. It brings the light of the gospel to those who embrace the truth. Then, as they learn and obey the commandments of

God, they will prosper. This promise has been recorded by prophets throughout time and in diverse places. Working with a will, those who accept the Father's plan gain a new appreciation of who they are and of their eternal worth. Righteousness, independence, thrift, industry, and self-reliance become their personal goals. These qualities transform lives. In time, in the Lord's "own way," the poor will no longer be poor.

Chapter 8

JOY COMETH IN THE MORNING

The title of this message is taken from Psalm 30:5: "Joy cometh in the morning." As I discussed this scripture with members of our family, they recalled that "men are, that they might have joy" (2 Nephi 2:25), but they had not pondered the intriguing concept that "joy cometh in the morning."

One of our family said, "News reports appear almost daily concerning people with problems of drugs, drinking, and emotional distress. How can they, and we, attain the joy spoken of in the scriptures?"

"The gospel of Jesus Christ offers hope," I answered. "It declares joy to be part of our divine destiny. And to experience joy in the morning becomes our special challenge. The true test is to be able to look in the mirror first thing in the morning and feel real joy."

One of our daughters, who had recently announced that she was expecting a new addition to the family, said, "But Dad, that's the hardest time of the day for me!"

"My dear ones," I replied, "in order to experience true joy in the morning, or at any time, at least three factors are needed. You need to feel good about the people with whom you live and work—your companions in life. You must feel good about yourself, not in any sense of conceit, but simply feel proper esteem for yourself. And possibly most important, you must feel good about your relation to God and sincerely love him."

As I counseled my family in that conversation, so we all might consider those three steps to achieve real joy in life.

First, joy in the morning begins with courtesy to companions.

When shades of slumber first admit the light of dawn, I reach gently for my beloved companion nearby. I gain sweet reassurance that all is well with her, even before my eyes are fully opened. That reminds me, incidentally, of advice given by President David O. McKay, who said, "During courtship we should keep our eyes wide open, but after marriage keep them half shut." (*Conference Report*, April 1956, p. 9.)

My sweetheart has done that. Through our many long years of postgraduate study, professional responsibilities, and a growing family, she did not complain. Recently I overheard a conversation she had with young mothers enduring similar stress. They asked her how she managed with ten children and a husband whose time to help was so limited. Kindness was reflected in her reply: "Through our struggling years I didn't expect much, so I was rarely disappointed."

She is special. With her, it is easy to obey the scriptural injunction to "live joyfully with the wife whom thou lovest all the days of [thy] life." (Ecclesiastes 9:9.)

Not everyone is blessed with such a wonderful companion — not yet anyway. Many who are married cannot be together as much as they would like. Thankfully, all can have companionship of family and friends.

Recently another General Authority was my partner for mission tours to dusty places. On occasion when I returned from a morning shower, I found to my surprise that this considerate companion had shined my shoes. Gratefully I wondered if each of the thirty thousand missionaries now laboring in the Lord's service would have been, and would be, as kind a friend as he was to me, thoughtfully rendering simple acts of courtesy to a companion.

Joy cometh in the morning to those who have earned the night's rest of a laborer. One of life's sweetest returns is the privilege of rendering significant service of worth to others. To be able to do for fellow human beings something they cannot do for themselves brings matchless satisfaction. Years of preparation are worth it.

Joy is also derived from church service. Alma expressed this thought: "That perhaps I may be an instrument in the hands of God to bring some soul to repentance . . . is my joy." (Alma 29:9.)

Through service in the temples, the concept of courtesy to companions can be nobly extended to those who have passed beyond the veil. The gospel brings glad tidings for the dead and a voice of gladness for the living and the dead—for all, glad tidings of great joy. (See D&C 128:19.)

Even when death's veil separates us from parents who gave so much that we might be, their righteous influence continues with us. And as they may watch from windows of heaven, their mornings will be brighter if they can truly say, as did the apostle John, "I have no greater joy than to hear that my children walk in truth." (3 John 1:4.)

Above all, courtesy to companions cannot be defiled by disobedience to the law of chastity. That sin is joy's deadly poison. The first morning's glance in the mirror cannot reflect joy if there is any recollection of misdeeds the night before. The surest step toward joy in the morning is virtue in the evening. Virtue includes courtesy to companions all day long.

Second, joy comes through feeling good about ourselves.

The second of our Lord's two great commandments carries a double charge: "Thou shalt love thy neighbour as thyself." (Matthew 22:39.) Therefore, love of companion is governed, in part, by esteem of self, and so is joy in the morning.

Each individual should understand the nature of his or her own soul. Profound insight is provided by this revelation: "For man is spirit. The elements are eternal, and spirit and element, inseparably connected, receive a fulness of joy; and when separated, man cannot receive a fulness of joy." (D&C 93:33-34.)

Therefore, both spiritual and physical elements must be nurtured if we are to earn proper self-esteem.

Spiritual self-esteem begins with the realization that each new morning is a gift from God. Even the air we breathe is a loving loan from him. He preserves us from day to day and supports us from one moment to another. (See Mosiah 2:21.) Therefore, our first noble deed of the morning should be a humble prayer of gratitude. Scripture counsels, "Pray unto God, and he will be favourable unto [you]: and [you] shall see his face with joy." (Job 33:26; see also Alma 34:21; 37:37.)

I did not fully appreciate the significance of prayerful greetings until I became a father myself. I am so grateful that our children have never given their mother or dad the silent treatment. Now I sense how our Heavenly Father may appreciate our prayers, morning and night. I can imagine also the pangs of his sorrow because of silence from any of his children. To me, such ingratitude seems comparable to sullen goldfish oblivious to kind providers who sprinkle food in their bowl. Indeed, those who pray can "worship God with exceedingly great joy." (Alma 45:1.)

I learned long ago that a period of uninterrupted scriptural study in the morning brings enduring enrichment. I feel as did Jeremiah: "Thy word was unto me the joy and rejoicing of mine heart." (Jeremiah 15:16.) Sacred scriptures have been repeatedly described as "glad tidings of great joy." (See, for example, Helaman 16:14; Mosiah 3:3; Alma 13:22; Luke 2:10.) As we learn and abide their teachings, that joy becomes part of our lives.

Joy cometh in the morning when personal talents are developed. Each of us is blessed with unique potential. I don't think I could get up early enough to become a portrait painter. But I have appreciated teachings since my earliest childhood from parents who knew the joy that good music brings. And some of the sweetest sounds in our home have been those from songs and instruments of children improving their talents.

Confidence to begin each morning ready to meet the challenges of the day comes from spiritual self-esteem.

Physical self-esteem also requires nurturing. Our bodies deserve thoughtful care. I echo this declaration of Paul: "Know ye not that ye are the temple of God, and that the Spirit of God dwelleth in you? If any man defile the temple of God, him shall God destroy; for the temple of God is holy, which temple ye are." (1 Corinthians 3:16-17.)

Physical conditioning from regular exercise is important. And we can do so much more to keep our bodies strong.

In 1833 the Prophet Joseph Smith received the Word of Wisdom by revelation. It includes these simple directives: We are not to drink alcohol, tea, or coffee, and we are not to use tobacco. Prophets in our generation have also told us to avoid harmful drugs. Today, medical science increasingly confirms the physical benefits of compliance with these teachings.

The damaging effects of alcohol are so widely known that additional comment is hardly needed. Harm inflicted by alcohol has been demonstrated, for example, by a study of the relationship between alcohol consumption among expectant mothers and the birth weight of their newborn infants. Findings published recently from the National Institutes of Health disclosed that consumption of one to two alcoholic drinks a day was associated with a substantially increased risk of producing a growth-retarded infant.[1]

Scientists now know that the smoking of tobacco is the number one preventable cause of death in all the world. It is the leading preventable cause of heart disease, lung disease, artery disease, and cancer.[2]

Still another report indicates that more than one-fourth of all deaths in the United States are now caused by conditions that physicians classify as addictive disorders.[3]

Obedience to the Word of Wisdom keeps one free from all such addictions. This protection is pronounced by covenant in the last verse of section 89 in the Doctrine and Covenants: "And I, the Lord, give unto them a promise, that the destroying angel shall pass by them, as the children of Israel, and not slay them." (D&C 89:21.)

This reference to the first Passover reminds us that, *in faith*, ancient Israel was obedient to the commandment to take blood and "strike it on the two side posts and on the upper door post of the houses. . . . And the blood shall be to you for a token upon the houses where ye are: and when I see the blood, I will pass over you, and the plague shall not . . . destroy you." (Exodus 12:7, 13.)

So, in faith, modern Israel is commanded to obey the Word of Wisdom. It becomes our token of a covenant with the Lord — a spiritual separator of covenant Israel from the rest of the world.

Joy cometh in the morning — to those who can stand before the mirror and feel clean, to those whose mouths are free from the taste of flavors forbidden by the Lord, to those whose spirits and bodies are free from feelings of self-remorse.

Third, the crowning attribute toward joy is love of God.

Even that first look in the mirror can be more enjoyable when we know we are created in his image. Each of us can say, as did the apostle Peter, "Thou hast made known to me the ways of life; thou shalt make me full of joy with thy countenance." (Acts 2:28; see also Psalm 16:11.)

God, who gave us life, also gave us commandments to live by so that we might have joy. They have been revealed periodically by prophets from the days of Adam to President Ezra Taft Benson. An ancient prophet wrote this expression: "Consider . . . the blessed and happy state of those that keep the commandments of God. For behold, they are blessed in all things, both temporal and spiritual." (Mosiah 2:41.)

For those who have not known his ways or who have strayed from them, remember, it is not too late to change. Blessings from faith and repentance can still be yours.

To those who feel defeated and downtrodden, look to the early hours of the day for your rescue. The Lord told us, "Cease to sleep longer than is needful; retire to thy bed early, that ye may not be weary; arise early, that your bodies and your minds may be invigorated." (D&C 88:124.)

The dawning of a brighter day heralds a time of forgiveness. Shadows of yesterday's grief melt in the rays of early morning's opportunity. Joy comes from our posterity, and we rejoice as they are blessed by the ordinances of salvation and exaltation.

Our family experienced that in a special way when our youngest daughter was sealed to her eternal companion in the holy temple. There to witness this event, along with other family members, were her parents and all eight of her older sisters and their husbands. For us, there was truly joy in the morning on that day. Then we really felt the scriptural truth, "Men are, that they might have joy." (2 Nephi 2:25.)

These experiences, glorious as they are, become but prelude to that great day ahead when the faithful will stand at the latter day upon the earth. They shall abide the Second Coming of the Lord and shall stand with him when he appears. (See Malachi 3:2-12; 3 Nephi 24:2-12.)

On that joyous morning, the mirror will reflect the miracle of the first resurrection. The faithful shall be crowned with glory, immortality, and eternal lives. (See D&C 75:5; 138:51.) Once again "morning stars [will] sing together, and ... all the sons [and daughters] of God [will] shout for joy!" (D&C 128:23; see also Job 38:7.) For on that morning, "the glory of the Lord shall be revealed, and all flesh shall see it together." (Isaiah 40:5; see also Ezekiel 20:48; Luke 3:6; D&C 101:23.)

NOTES

1. J. L. Mills, B. I. Braubard, E. E. Harley, G. G. Rhoads, and H. W. Berendes, "Maternal Alcohol Consumption and Birth Weight: How Much Drinking During Pregnancy Is Safe?," *Journal of the American Medical Association* 252 (October 12, 1984): 1875.

2. W. Pollin and R. T. Ravenholt, "Tobacco Addiction and Tobacco Mortality," *Journal of the American Medical Association* 252 (November 23, 1984): 2851. *1986 Heart Facts*, American Heart Association, p. 16. *The Health Consequences of Smoking: A Report of the Surgeon General*, publication DHHS (PHS) 84-50204, U.S. Department of Health and Human Services, Office on Smoking and Health, 1983.

3. Pollin and Ravenholt, "Tobacco Addiction and Tobacco Mortality," 252:2849.

Chapter 9

LOVE THY NEIGHBOR

The Lord's concern for the one is evident in many ways. In chapter 15 of Luke alone, three illustrations are given, all pertaining to the retrieval of one who is lost. The parables of the lost sheep, the piece of silver, and the prodigal son, all emphasize the anxiety our Lord has for each individual soul.

A statement of the Lord's prophet on the earth today conveys that continuing concern. The First Presidency recently said, "We rejoice in the blessings that come of membership and activity in this church, whose head is the Son of God, the Lord Jesus Christ." Those not receiving the blessings of full activity in the Church are invited to "come back and feast at the table of the Lord, and taste again the sweet and satisfying fruits of fellowship with the Saints." (*Church News,* December 22, 1985, p. 3.)

Sometimes in our zeal to do right, we may stumble over our own shoes. Our efforts to do good may be undermined unknowingly by labels we apply. Labels are important. We tag a special package "fragile." We name a beautiful flower a rose, notwithstanding the fact that "a rose by any other name would smell as sweet."(William Shakespeare, *Romeo and Juliet,* Act II, scene 2.)

As we study the Old Testament, we learn the symbolic significance of names given to the great patriarchs. Abram, for example, had a name that means "exalted father." Just as he was getting used to that name, after ninety-nine years, the Lord changed it from Abram to Abraham, to indicate he would be more than an exalted father. He would become "a father of many nations." (See Genesis 17:1-5.)

Gabriel, magnified by many heavenly errands, bears a name that means "man of God."

The name Elijah, meaning "my God is Jehovah," has components of the names of both Elohim and Jehovah. Bearing a name signifying the Father and the Son, Elijah was the one entrusted with the keys "to turn the hearts of the fathers to the children, and the children to the fathers." (D&C 110:15.)

A child who is slow of speech may speak with even less assurance if he is declared a stammerer by others. In fact, some evidence suggests that stuttering is aggravated merely by labeling one a stutterer.

Unkind words exchanged between people can injure deeply, especially if discourteous labels are applied in the process. People tend to become what is expected of them. Labels convey those expectations. Pigeons feel comfortable in designated pigeonholes, and mail may be categorized when sorted into labeled slots. But people can be offended when labeled or classified. Yet we are so prone to label one another. "Smoker," "drinker," "inactive," "liberal," "unorthodox" are but a few terms applied, as though our thinking could not separate the doer from the deed.

May I quote excerpts from a letter to illustrate how harmful such labels can be:

> I'm an ex-Mormon. I've been "officially" out of the Church now for 6 months. . . . Despite everything, I loved the LDS Church. . . . I would just like the LDS people to know how an ex-Mormon feels and why I left the Church. . . .
>
> I found out that I was on the inactive list. . . . I was so hurt, I felt like my own church slapped me in the face. . . .
>
> It was when I needed the strength of the Church so much that it lost me. I had no visits from home teachers or visiting teachers, no calls from Relief Society. . . .
>
> I miss the Church. I miss the serenity I felt. . . . But as much as I miss it, I'm too afraid to go back. Too afraid of being hurt, too afraid of feeling "ugly and unpopular." (*The Latter-day Sentinel*, July 14, 1984, p. 2.)

In the eyes of God, all are his children. All are brothers and sisters. Millions who have joined the Church have witnessed to the Lord at the time of their baptism their willingness to take upon themselves his name and keep his commandments. Having entered the first gate, that of baptism, to embark along the strait and narrow path, members of the Church may progress along the way toward salvation and exaltation. But all are unique. We each progress at our own pace. Each is a choice soul, precious in the sight of the Lord, regardless of struggles from failure or challenges from unwise deeds. Many, if not most, of us will slip and fall somewhere along the way.

I hope we can teach every leader in the Church to love and lift all members, but especially those who have stumbled along this pathway. Leaders stand at a higher level of perception and can look back on those making the climb to see more clearly those in distress. "For if they fall, the one will lift up his fellow: but woe to him that is alone when he falleth: for he hath not another to help him up." (Ecclesiastes 4:10.)

In the future, I hope we can lift more people back on the path. Prevention is better than treatment of any illness. When interviews disclose even the slightest symptoms of spiritual sickness, help rendered then may be most therapeutic. I believe this is what the Lord meant when he taught us, through his prophet, to "lift up the hands which hang down, and the feeble knees; and make straight paths for your feet." (Hebrews 12:12-13.) For that correct path leads to the glorious gate that enables blessings of the priesthood to come into our lives, the gate of the temple. This is the ultimate reason for our membership in the Church, that we may enjoy all the blessings there for us and our families.

Obstacles along the way, such as habituation to tobacco or to stimulating drinks such as coffee and tea, need not raise artificial barriers to stand between us as brothers and sisters, or between an individual and the fulfillment of his or her own potential.

Years ago, for example, I was given a home teaching assignment to a special couple. A faithful, wonderful wife welcomed us to their home while her husband retreated to a small room filled with amateur radio equipment. But our concern for him was great enough to tolerate the dense smoke of his cigars as he reluctantly responded to our questions about the principles of radio operation. As our regular visits continued, earlier barriers became melted into bonds of a dear friendship. Our wives became fast friends too. The sweetness of his soul began to emerge. He refined his life. Now, over thirty years later, we look back on his distinguished service as a stake president, mission president, and temple president. And recently I had the great privilege of ordaining this dear friend of mine a patriarch.

Paul wrote to the Galatians: "Brethren, if a man be overtaken in a fault, ye which are spiritual, restore such an one in the spirit of meekness. . . . Bear ye one another's burdens, and so fulfil the law of Christ. . . . As we have therefore opportunity, let us do good unto all men, especially unto them who are of the household of faith." (Galatians 6:1-2, 10.)

A wife grieves because of errant activities of her husband. Parents sorrow when their loved ones go astray. But scriptures hold great promise, particularly for those who have been taught the gospel earlier in life. "Train up a child in the way he should go," the proverb states, "and when he is old, he will not depart from it." (Proverbs 22:6.)

Job expressed hope with this analogy: "For there is hope of a tree, if it be cut down, that it will sprout again, and that the tender branch thereof will not cease. Though the root thereof wax old in the earth, and the stock thereof die in the ground; yet through the scent of water it will bud, and bring forth boughs like a plant." (Job 14:7-9.)

That scent of water is the wonderful refreshment of love. Most who have separated themselves from full fellowship in the Church have done so not because of doctrinal disputations but because of hurt, neglect, or lack of love. Progress toward full participation in the blessings of the gospel needs no new programs, only new vision of love, which can be rendered best by friends and neighbors.

Someone asked the Savior: "Master, which is the great commandment in the law?" Jesus responded, "Thou shalt love the Lord thy God with all thy heart, and with all thy soul, and with all thy mind. This is the first and great commandment. And the second is like unto it, Thou shalt love thy neighbour as thyself. On these two commandments hang all the law and the prophets." (Matthew 22:36-40.)

Quick and easy ways to come back cannot be packaged at Church headquarters and delivered to local priesthood leaders. Love cannot be conveyed remotely, even with new technology. These two great commandments must be applied by leaders of the Church locally. The way to build the Church in each stake and mission is to "preach [the] gospel . . . and . . . cause [the] church to be established." (D&C 28:8.)

When that happens, great blessings of eternal worth will result, "for whoso is faithful unto the obtaining these two priesthoods of which I have spoken, and the magnifying their calling, are sanctified by the Spirit unto the renewing of their bodies. They become the sons of Moses and of Aaron and the seed of Abraham, and the church and kingdom, and the elect of God." The scripture promises further, "They who receive this priesthood receive me, saith the Lord; for he that receiveth my servants receiveth me; and he that receiveth me receiveth my Father; and he that receiveth my Father receiveth my Father's kingdom; therefore all that my Father hath shall be given unto him." (D&C 84:33-38.)

Such blessings of supernal significance are really worth our efforts, for ourselves and our neighbors. Priesthood quorums and the sisters of the Relief Society are an indispensable part of this preparation. Their agendas should be focused more on our Father's business of brotherhood and sisterhood and of blessings than on disputations.

Strength bonded in mutual commitment is envisioned in this passage from the Book of Mormon: "They were all young men, and they were exceedingly valiant for courage, and also for strength and activity; but behold, this was not all—they were men who were true at all times in whatsoever thing they were entrusted. Yea, they were men of truth and soberness, for they had been taught to keep the commandments of God and to walk uprightly before him." (Alma 53:20-21.)

In the church of our loving Lord, we all need each other. Paul explained this by likening the Saints to parts of the body: "If the foot shall say, Because I am not the hand, I am not of the body; is it therefore not of the body? And if the ear shall say, Because I am not the eye, I am not of the body; is it therefore not of the body?.... And the eye cannot say unto the hand, I have no need of thee: nor again the head to the feet, I have no need of you.... Now ye are the body of Christ, and members in particular." (1 Corinthians 12:15-16, 21, 27.)

As we fortify ourselves for our mighty redeeming tasks, may we heed this inspired prayer from the Book of Mormon: "O Lord, wilt thou grant unto us that we may have success in bringing [our brothers and sisters] again unto thee in Christ. Behold, O Lord, their souls are precious, and many of them are our brethren; therefore, give unto us, O Lord, power and wisdom that we may bring these, our brethren, again unto thee." (Alma 31:34-35.)

Let us unlabel our brothers and sisters. They are not strangers, "but fellowcitizens with the saints, and of the household of God." (Ephesians 2:19.) Let us all learn to love God and one another. Obedience to these two great commandments will crown our efforts with success. "Verily, thus saith the Lord, I say unto you, if those who call themselves by my name and are [trying] to be my saints, if they will do my will and keep my commandments ... they may be prepared for that which is in store for a time to come." (D&C 125:2.)

That time will be glorious, especially when shared with all the sheep of the fold, with none lost. We shall bless the lives of our families, friends, and neighbors as we help them prepare for the great day of the Lord, which is nigh.

Chapter 10

TRUTH AND MORE

When I was in medical school, I was taught that one must never touch the human heart, for if one did, it would stop beating. That was the limit of our knowledge of the truth then. I remember our first experiments on animals during which we tenderly dared to incise the chest and open the pericardium (the sac around the heart) only after injecting novocaine to anesthetize the heart so that it "might not know" we were coming. It worked. Subsequently, we found that the heart continued to function even if we didn't anesthetize it. It beat merrily on its way even if we touched it, held it, or stitched it. As a result of these early and later more detailed experiments and the work of many others, all designed to find more of the truth, safe surgery on the heart has now become routine in most nations of the earth.

That background, drawn from my own personal experience, may serve to distinguish "relative" from "absolute" truth. In fact, early in my professional training, one instructor said that everything taught in medical school should have a sign posted on it: "This is our present understanding of the truth — until it is later shown to be false."

Of course, the truth isn't "relative." It is man's understanding of the truth that is really "relative."

Researchers realize that only a small sample of the totality of "absolute" truth is already known. Therein lies the allure of research. Few rewards are as exciting as the discovery of truth, through research well performed. But truth proclaimed by Deity is as absolute as Deity. It is defined as "knowledge of things as they are, and as they were, and as they are to come." (D&C 93:24.)

The glory of truth is revealed in these words of the Master: "If ye continue in my word, then are ye my disciples indeed; and ye shall know the truth, and the truth shall make you free." (John 8:31-32.) Truth literally makes us free from the bondage that ignorance brings.

Many great people have been imbued with a passion for truth. One of these was John Jaques, who was born in England January 7, 1827, a son of Wesleyan Methodist parents. His father must have been rather stern with the boy, because the record of his childhood memories included notation of his being hidden by his mother mercifully in the folds of her apron when his father wanted to whip him. As a boy, John gathered horse manure along the road and sold it to farmers for fertilizer. A good cartload brought four shillings.

In his youth, he recorded that he was earnestly seeking the true religion. After intensive study with missionaries who taught him the gospel, he was baptized in 1845, at age eighteen, and became a member of The Church of Jesus Christ of Latter-day Saints.

John's austere father, upset upon hearing this news, wrote: "I wished you . . . to attend the Wesleyan Chapel. They [the Mormons] do not teach you . . . [to] honor and obey your parents. I . . . hope you will give up the idea of belonging to such a party. . . . It is fiction."

John's reply, written March 14, 1847, when he was but twenty years of age, included these words: "Dear Father: I would pray . . . that I may be led and guided into all truth that I may understand the things of the Kingdom of God and carry my ideas to you . . . and be enabled to understand truth. . . . Before I conclude I will . . . bear . . . humble testimony to the truth of the work which the Lord has commenced. . . . Since I [joined the Church] my eyes have been opened, and I have been able to understand the truth. I can bear testimony to the truth . . . of the doctrines . . . in the Church of Jesus Christ of Latter-day Saints."

John then likened the truth of the gospel to a diamond, while comparing "the low smattering of education . . . of religionists" to "the common pebble of a rivulet." (Stella Jaques Bell, *Life History and Writings of John Jaques,* pp. 19-21.)

At age twenty-three, John Jaques wrote these immortal lines:

> Oh say, what is truth? 'Tis the fairest gem
> That the riches of worlds can produce,
> And priceless the value of truth will be when
> The proud monarch's costliest diadem
> Is counted but dross and refuse.
>
> Yes, say, what is truth? 'Tis the brightest prize
> To which mortals or Gods can aspire.
> Go search in the depths where it glittering lies,
> Or ascend in pursuit to the loftiest skies:
> 'Tis an aim for the noblest desire.
>
> The sceptre may fall from the despot's grasp,
> When with winds of stern justice he copes.
> But the pillar of truth will endure to the last,
> And its firm-rooted bulwarks outstand the rude blast
> And the wreck of the fell tryant's hopes.
>
> Then say, what is truth? 'Tis the last and the first,
> For the limits of time it steps o'er.
> Though the heavens depart and the earth's fountains burst,
> Truth, the sum of existence, will weather the worst,
> Eternal unchanged, evermore.
> (*Hymns*, no. 272)

Brother Jaques spent his last years in the Church Historian's Office, where he labored as an assistant to the historian from 1889 until his death June 1, 1900.

It is of interest that earlier, as an elder, John Jaques served as a missionary at Stratford-upon-Avon, the home of William Shakespeare. We recall Shakespeare's penchant for truth. This statement was made through his character Polonius:

> This above all: To thine own self be true,
> And it must follow, as the night the day,
> Thou canst not then be false to any man.
> (*Hamlet*, Act I, scene 3.)

Perhaps less known are these lines spoken by Isabella in the fifth act of Shakespeare's *Measure for Measure:*

> This is all as true as it is strange.
> Nay, it is ten times true, for truth is truth
> To the end of reckoning.

That expression closely mirrors the teaching of the Lord: "My . . . truth abideth and hath no end." (D&C 88:66.)

From the charter of Duke University in North Carolina, we read:

> The aims of Duke University are to assert a faith in the eternal union of knowledge and religion set forth in the teachings and character of Jesus Christ, the Son of God; to advance learning in all likeness of truth; to defend scholarship against all false notions and ideals; to develop a Christian love of freedom and truth; to promote a sincere spirit of tolerance; to discourage all partisan and sectarian strife; and to render the largest permanent service to the individual, the state, the nation, and the church. Unto these ends shall the affairs of this university always be administered.

The search for truth is not just institutional; it is also individual. Thirty years ago, as we were embarking on an uncharted sea early in the development of human open-heart surgery, I scheduled only one such operation a month. Each operation was a skirmish with terror, usually bringing us face-to-face with death, with the unknown, and with limitations imposed by our own ignorance. That confrontation forced us to return to the laboratory to overcome the inadequacies encountered during the previous experience. Then, when we were fortified and prepared by solving a specific problem, we would enter again the whirlpool of another experience, learning little by little some of the truth upon which the principles of safe open-heart surgery could one day stand.

Truth was there all the time. It was absolute—part of the

incontrovertibility of divine law that we had to know if we were to succeed. As we moved toward that light, we found truth to give reproducibility and safety where once in darkness there lurked the specters of fear, chance, and disaster. I learned the remarkable potential for truth. It is a powerful sword—an instrument that can be wielded just like a surgeon's knife. It can be guided well to bless. But it can also be crudely applied to wound, to cripple, to damage, and even to destroy.

May I give you an illustration? Imagine a surgeon who has just operated upon a patient and found cancer invading vital organs of the body. It is widespread and beyond cure. With this knowledge, the surgeon approaches the family and the patient and coldly announces that the patient has advanced cancer, that he is beyond hope and doomed to die. While discharging his duty to share that information, the surgeon has told the truth, but with utter abandon he has walked away from the turmoil that truth has left in its wake.

Another surgeon, with that same information and with compassion, approaches the family with truth *and more*. He speaks the truth and then mercifully indicates that, even though the road ahead will be difficult and challenging, the patient and the family will not be forsaken. They will be supported with all the resources available to him as their caring physician.

Another scene with which I am very familiar may illustrate further. A doctor may tell a patient with terminal heart disease that the patient's heart is worn out and no repairs are possible. The condition is beyond hope of significant medical or surgical assistance, and nothing more can be done. The doctor then discharges the patient from his care. The truth has been spoken, but no more. Another physician administering truth *and more* adds his pledge to ease the burden as much as his abilities allow.

These two illustrations depict the fact that, important as truth is, often we need truth *and more*.

Emily Dickinson expressed this concept poignantly: "The truth must dazzle gradually, or every man be blind."

As a slogan that encourages truth *and more*, I like the four-way test of Rotary International:

1. Is it the truth?
2. Is it fair to all concerned?
3. Will it build goodwill and better friendships?
4. Will it be beneficial to all?

In holy writ, the word *truth* is coupled with expressions of *mercy* in the same verse of scripture forty-seven times. *Truth* is joined with forms of *right* or *righteousness* in forty-two passages of scripture.

The psalmist wrote, for example: "Mercy and truth are met together; righteousness and peace have kissed each other." This verse is then followed by the prophecy of the coming of the Book of Mormon: "Truth shall spring out of the earth; and righteousness shall look down from heaven." (Psalm 85:10-11.)

A similar message comes from the Lord through the book of Moses: "Righteousness will I send down out of heaven; and truth will I send forth out of the earth, to bear testimony of mine Only Begotten." (Moses 7:62.)

We too might measure truth with the standard of mercy, if we are obedient to these passages from Proverbs: "Do they not err that devise evil? but mercy and truth shall be to them that devise good." (Proverbs 14:22.) "By mercy and truth iniquity is purged." (Proverbs 16:6.)

Those privileged to hold membership in the Church in which we claim testimony-bearing and covenant-keeping might well remember this psalm: "All the paths of the Lord are mercy and truth unto such as keep his covenant and his testimonies." (Psalm 25:10.) The psalmist added this observation: "But thou, O Lord, art a God full of compassion, and gracious, long-suffering, and plenteous in mercy and truth." (Psalm 86:15.) Otherwise, the sword of truth, cutting and sharp as a surgeon's scalpel, might not be governed by righteousness or by mercy, but might be misused carelessly to embarrass, debase, or deceive others.

94

This reminds me of a personal experience. I was serving (at some personal sacrifice) as a consultant to the United States government at its National Center for Disease Control in Atlanta, Georgia. Once while awaiting a taxi to take me to the airport after our meetings were over, I stretched out on the lawn to soak in a few welcome rays of sunshine before returning to the winter weather of Utah's January. Later, in the mail I received a photograph, taken by a photographer with a telephoto lens, capturing my moment of basking on the lawn. Under it a caption read "Governmental consultant at the National Center." The picture was true, the caption was true, but the truth was used to promote a false impression. Yes, truth can even be used to convey a lie.

Indeed, in some instances, the merciful companion to truth is silence. Some truths are best left unsaid. My mother expressed that thought to me often with this simple advice: "Russell, if you can't say something nice about someone, say nothing." I might add, incidentally, that her injunction became a real challenge to me, for my entire professional life required my telling each patient about the abnormalities that he or she possessed.

We live in a day when politicians occasionally dig for "truth" that would degrade an opponent. We live in a time when some journalists may not be content to *report* the news, but instead work to *create* news through journalistic techniques designed to demean another's work of worth. We now live in a season in which some self-serving historians grovel for "truth" that would defame the dead and the defenseless. Some may be tempted to undermine what is sacred to others, or diminish the esteem of honored names, or demean the efforts of revered individuals. They seem to forget that the greatness of the very lives they examine has given the historian the pedestal from which such work may have any interest.

But these temptations are not new. Regarding them, President Stephen L Richards expressed similar concerns more than thirty years ago:

THE POWER WITHIN US

If a man of history has secured over the years a high place in the esteem of his countrymen and fellow men and has become imbedded in their affections, it has seemingly become a pleasing pastime for researchers and scholars to delve into the past of such a man, discover, if may be, some of his weaknesses and then write a book exposing hitherto unpublished alleged factual findings, all of which tends to rob the historic character of the idealistic esteem and veneration in which he may have been held through the years.

... If an historic character has made a great contribution to country and society, and if his name and his deeds have been used over the generations to foster high ideals of character and service, what good is to be accomplished by digging out of the past and exploiting weaknesses, which perhaps a generous contemporary public forgave?

... Perhaps, with propriety, we might look into ... their objectives in destroying this idealism for our heroes and great men of history. Perhaps ... their investigation and writing are prompted by a desire to show that men can be human, with human frailties, and still be great. If they were to say that that was their purpose, I would be inclined to doubt them, and much more inclined to believe that their writings were prompted by a desire to make money out of sensational, unsavory disclosures. (*Where Is Wisdom?*, p. 155.)

Extortion by threat of disclosing truth is labeled "blackmail." Is sordid disclosure for personal attention or financial gain not closely related?

Paul perceived the wise judgment needed in wielding the powerful sword of truth as he taught: "Study to shew thyself approved unto God ... *rightly dividing* the word of truth." (2 Timothy 2:15; emphasis added.) Rightly dividing the word of truth portends responsibility to apportion it wisely, taking care not to injure or destroy. Thus, many scriptures caution the need to join truth together with righteousness. Here are six examples:

David my father ... walked before thee in truth, and in righteousness. (1 Kings 3:6.)

Who shall dwell in thy holy hill? He that walketh uprightly, and worketh righteousness, and speaketh the truth in his heart. He that backbiteth not with his tongue, nor doeth evil to his neighbour, nor taketh up a reproach against his neighbor. (Psalm 15:1-3.)

Christ . . . is the word of truth and righteousness. (Alma 38:9.)

They did begin to keep his statutes and commandments, and to walk in truth and uprightness before him. (Helaman 6:34.)

The fruit of the Spirit is in all goodness and righteousness and truth. (Ephesians 5:9.)

Let every man beware lest he do that which is not in truth and righteousness before me. (D&C 50:9.)

Another pertains to the second coming of the Savior:

Thus saith the Lord of hosts, . . . they shall be my people, and I will be their God, in truth and in righteousness. (Zechariah 8:7-8.)

Don't misunderstand. I do not decry the revealing of negative information per se. A prosecutor who uncovers an embezzlement combines both truth and justice. A journalist who rightly reports betrayal of official trust combines truth with righteousness. Physicians who determined that old-fashioned bloodletting did more harm than good strengthened truth with light.

But any who are tempted to rake through the annals of history, to combine truth with *unrighteousness*, or truth with the intent to defame or destroy, should hearken to this warning verse of scripture: "The righteousness of God [is] revealed from faith to faith: as it is written, The just shall live by faith. For the wrath of God is revealed from heaven against all ungodliness and unrighteousness of men, who hold the truth in unrighteousness." (Romans 1:17-18.)

Those who, because of "truth," may be tempted to become dissenters against the Lord and his anointed should weigh carefully their action as they read this sacred scripture: "These dissenters, having the same instruction and the same information . . . yea, having been instructed in the same knowledge

97

of the Lord, nevertheless, it is strange to relate, not long after their dissensions they became more hardened and impenitent, and . . . wicked . . . entirely forgetting the Lord their God." (Alma 47:36.)

When teachers and writers leave the lofty ethics of their honored professions, passing from legitimate reporting to feasting on sensational and pointless disclosures that appeal temporarily to a flattering few, their work slants more toward gossip than gospel. Even worse, if they "lift up [their] heel against mine anointed, saith the Lord, . . . their basket shall not be full, their houses and their barns shall perish, and they themselves shall be despised by those that flattered them." (D&C 121:16, 20.)

Scriptures teach us that the pleasantries of prosperity, if tainted by seeds of selfishness and dissension against the Lord (or his anointed), comprise a dangerous combination. These verses are a solemn warning to us all:

> The very time when he doth prosper his people, yea, in the increase of their fields, their flocks and their herds, and in gold, and in silver, and in all manner of precious things . . . for the welfare and happiness of his people; yea, then is the time that they do harden their hearts, and do forget the Lord their God, and do trample under their feet the Holy One—yea, and this because of their ease, and their exceedingly great prosperity. . . . Yea, how quick to be lifted up in pride; yea, how quick to boast, and do all manner of that which is iniquity; and how slow are they to remember the Lord their God, and to give ear unto his counsels, yea, how slow to walk in wisdom's paths! Behold, they do not desire that the Lord their God, who hath created them, should rule and reign over them; notwithstanding his great goodness and his mercy towards them, they do set at naught his counsels, and they will not that he should be their guide. (Helaman 12:2-6.)

If true and righteous people are silent, those who use truth in unrighteousness will prevail. Speaking from his viewpoint in history, Winston Churchill observed, "How the malice of the wicked was reinforced by the weakness of the virtuous . . . how the middle course adopted from desires for safety and a quiet life may be found to lead direct to the bull's-eye of disaster." (*The Gathering Storm*, pp. 15-16.)

We must realize that we are at war. The war began before the world was, and it will continue. The forces of the adversary are extant upon the earth. All of our virtuous motives, if transmitted only by inertia and timidity, are no match for the resolute wickedness of those who oppose us.

Every Latter-day Saint should think, speak, and write throughout the world in consonance with this proverb: "For my mouth shall speak truth; and wickedness is an abomination to my lips. All the words of my mouth are in righteousness; there is nothing . . . perverse in them." (Proverbs 8:7-8).

The word *truth* is used 435 times in the scriptures. I have studied each of them. In 374 of those instances, truth is coupled in the same verse with some form of a strengthening term, such as:

spirit	59	loving kindness	11
mercy(-iful)	47	wisdom	10
right(-eousness)	42	soberness	5
holy(-iness)	36	sanctified	4
judgment	23	kindness	3
light	23	sincerity	3
grace	22	free	2
good(-ly, -liness)	21	godliness	2
love	18	long-suffering	1
peace	16	valiant	1
just(-ice)	13		
faith(-fulness)	12	Total:	374*

The majority of the scriptural references exemplify the importance of truth *and more*.

What do these figures tell us? Truth *and more* bring more than truth alone. Just as oxen may be equally yoked together to accomplish what one could not do alone, so the power of

---

* In some verses, there is duplication of these listed terms.

truth is augmented if equally yoked together with righteousness or with mercy or with the spirit of love.

Truth, like justice, can be harsh and unforgiving when not tempered with mercy. But when truth is magnified by mercy or rectified by righteousness, it can be converted from a force to destroy to a force to bless — whether at home, at church, or in our work.

Ours is the glorious privilege of searching for truth, teaching the truth, and applying it righteously in service to others. We are sons and daughters of God engaged in his work. May we each turn in unity toward a commitment to truth *and more* in our homes and wherever we walk.

Chapter 11

KEYS OF THE PRIESTHOOD

You know how valuable keys can be. Many, if not most, people carry keys in their pockets. But some keys, though invisible, are far more important than those that are tangible. They are precious and powerful. Some can lock and unlock in heaven as well as on earth. I speak of keys of the priesthood.

Prior to my call to the Twelve, I served as a medical doctor and surgeon. I had earned two doctoral degrees. I had been certified by two specialty boards. That long preparation had consumed many years, yet it carried no legal permission. Keys were required. They were held by authorities of the state government and the hospitals in which I desired to work. Once those holding proper authority exercised those keys by granting me a license and permission, then I could perform operations. In return, I was obligated to obey the law, to be loyal, and to understand and not abuse the power of a surgeon's knife. The important steps of preparation, permission, and obligation likewise pertain to other occupations.

Why is the power to act in the name of God more important than those keys? Because it is of eternal significance. We should understand the source of our authority and something about the keys that control its power. They may benefit every man, woman, and child who now lives, who has lived, and who yet will live upon the earth.

Let us consider keys of the priesthood through three scenes of history: in ancient days, during the Lord's mortal ministry, and in modern times.

SCENE ONE: ANCIENT DAYS

Scene one pertains to keys of the priesthood in ancient days, even before the creation of the earth. We existed then as spirit children of God. Abraham was one of us. He was told that he was among rulers chosen even before he was born. (See Abraham 3:23.) Scriptures also relate that the Lord God foreordained priests prepared from the foundation of the world according to his foreknowledge. Thus, our calling to the holy priesthood was foreseen before we were born. (See Alma 13:1-5.)

We know that Adam received priesthood authority before the world was formed. (See *Teachings of the Prophet Joseph Smith*, pp. 157-58, 166-67. See also D&C 78:16.)

The potential of the priesthood is so vast that our comprehension of it is a challenge. The Prophet Joseph Smith declared, "The Priesthood is an everlasting principle, and existed with God from eternity, and will to eternity." (*Teachings of the Prophet Joseph Smith*, p. 157.)

President Brigham Young explained that the priesthood is "the law by which the worlds are, were, and will continue for ever and ever." (*Discourses of Brigham Young*, 1941 ed., p. 130.)

Priesthood is the authority of God delegated to man to minister for the salvation of men. According to President Joseph F. Smith, "The power of directing these labors constitutes the *keys* of the Priesthood." (*Improvement Era* 14 [January 1901]: 230.)

Many in scene one held those keys, including Abraham, Isaac, Jacob, Joseph, Moses, Elias, and Elijah.

SCENE TWO: THE MORTAL MINISTRY OF THE LORD

Scene two pertains to keys of the priesthood during the mortal ministry of the Lord. Jesus revealed the extent of priesthood authority. To his apostles he said, "I will give unto thee the keys of the kingdom of heaven: and whatsoever thou shalt bind on earth shall be bound in heaven: and whatsoever thou shalt loose on earth shall be loosed in heaven." (Matthew 16:19; see also D&C 128:10.)

Within a week of that promise, Jesus took Peter, James, and John to a high mountain, where keys of the priesthood were bestowed upon them, under divine direction, by Moses and Elijah (Elias). (See Matthew 17:1-5.) The Master then reminded his disciples of their sacred calls to the holy apostleship: "Ye have not chosen me, but I have chosen you, and ordained you." (John 15:16; see also D&C 7:7.) Jesus not only called and ordained men, but he also taught them their duties.

After Christ was crucified, and even before the early apostles completed their labors, the apostasy began. This occurred as prophesied when priesthood authority was abused and sacred ordinances were defiled.

SCENE THREE: MODERN TIMES

With scenes one and two as background, let us consider scene three—the modern times in which we live. After centuries of apostasy, keys of the priesthood have again been restored. Under that authority, we have had hands laid upon our heads.

Obligations pertain to those who *give* and to those who *receive* ordinations or calls. Perhaps that can be explained by the following example:

I hold a set of keys to an automobile. In your mind, let them represent keys to something of value in your life—a tractor, an implement, or a powerful instrument. If I give keys to you, I have certain obligations, and you have certain obligations. For me as the giver, I have a duty toward your success. Should you fail, in a measure I have failed. So I must teach and train adequately to ensure your personal safety and, at the same time, safeguard precious property you are to use. For you as the receiver, obligations accompany the keys. You must know applicable laws and obey them. Loyalty is expected. And you should understand the power of your instrument. Obedience, loyalty, and understanding are implicit with your acceptance of those keys.

Now apply the same principles to keys of the priesthood. Each stake president, quorum president, and bishop holds keys of presidency. Their keys control the power of their particular unit of the Church. Those leaders may not only call and release, but they must also train and bear sacred responsibility in order that the mission of the Church be accomplished. Those individuals who receive ordinations or callings have obligations of obedience, loyalty, and understanding.

Obedience to law first and foremost means keeping the commandments of God. By so doing, one becomes worthy to receive personal revelation. Those who receive the Melchizedek Priesthood are under solemn oath and covenant to "live by every word that proceedeth forth from the mouth of God." (D&C 84:44.)

Loyalty is vital. Loyalty to him who has keys to call and to release, even though he is an imperfect human being, will develop unity essential to success. (See D&C 124:45-46.) The Lord defined this reality when he said: "Israel shall be saved in mine own due time; and by the keys which I have given shall they be led." (D&C 35:25.)

To understand the power of the priesthood, we must know its limitations. If a youth drives an automobile recklessly, future permission from parents is likely to be denied. And if priesthood power is abused, "the Spirit of the Lord is grieved; and when it is withdrawn, Amen to the priesthood or the authority of that man." (D&C 121:37.)

To understand the power of the priesthood, we must know the divinity of its restoration in these latter days. In 1820, our Heavenly Father and his Son, Jesus Christ, appeared to the Prophet Joseph Smith. In 1829, John the Baptist conferred the Aaronic Priesthood upon Joseph Smith and Oliver Cowdery. (See D&C 13; 27:8; also JS–History 1:69, 72.) Shortly thereafter they received the Melchizedek Priesthood under the hands of Peter, James, and John. (See D&C 27:11-12.)

Later, the Lord spoke to Joseph and Oliver of others to whom specific priesthood keys had been committed. Each, in turn, conferred these keys: Moroni, keys of the Book of Mormon (see D&C 27:5); Moses, keys of the gathering of Israel and the leading of the ten tribes (see D&C 110:11); Elias, keys of the restoration of all things (see D&C 27:6), including the Abrahamic covenant (see D&C 110:12); and Elijah, keys of the sealing power (see D&C 27:9; 110:13-16; 128:21).

Joseph Smith conferred all keys on all of the Twelve. (See Joseph Fielding Smith, *Doctrines of Salvation* 3:154-56.) In turn, keys have been transferred to present leaders. Today, President Ezra Taft Benson actively holds every restored key held by "all those who have received a dispensation at any time from the beginning of the creation." (D&C 112:31; emphasis added. See also D&C 128:18.)

Surely a sacred moment of my life occurred April 12, 1984, when the First Presidency and members of the Quorum of the Twelve Apostles laid their hands upon my head. As had been done for others before me, all the keys of the priesthood were conferred. As it is with each member of the Quorum of the Twelve, some keys are not used until called upon by the Lord, or as directed by his senior apostle.

I feel the weight of responsibility and the burden of timeless trust. I know those keys have been restored "for the last days and for the last time." (D&C 112:30.) I am deeply grateful that I bear the priesthood and that each of us who bears the priesthood was foreordained from the foundation of the world for that responsibility. (See Alma 13:1-5.)

As a symbol of gratitude, I have penned a few lines as the concluding portion of this message. A verse for each of three scenes of history may summarize my remarks. To this song, written to some music from Wales,[1] I have assigned an ancient title, "Hosanna," the prayerful shout of fervent praise:

> Through time's immortal endless stay
> In love he guides our way
> Beyond the realms of heaven's beam,

105

THE POWER WITHIN US

Our great God, Elohim.
Hosanna to his holy name —
Our fathers' God is still the same.

That holy night in Bethlehem
His Son was born among men
To ransom from a timeless grave,
Each child of God to save.
Hosanna to his holy name —
Our fathers' God is still the same.

His priesthood power restored to earth
To bless each soul given birth.
Our song of prayer to him we raise,
Proclaiming joy and praise.
Hosanna to his holy name —
Our fathers' God is still the same.

Amen, amen, amen, amen.[2]

May we be true to the trust he has given to us who bear the holy priesthood and hold its sacred keys.

NOTES

1. "Tydi A Roddaist" by Arwell Hughes (copyright 1938). Gratitude is expressed to Mr. Hughes for permission to use his music with these words, and to Barry D. R. Whittaker, president of the Cardiff Wales Stake, for his assistance.
2. Copyright 1987 Russell M. Nelson.

Chapter 12

LESSONS FROM EVE

Without women, the whole purpose of the creation of this world would be in vain. This truth we learn from the scriptures.

Before the world was formed, the Lord Jesus Christ was Jehovah, "the Great I Am, . . . the beginning and the end, . . . [who] looked upon the wide expanse of eternity, and all the seraphic hosts of heaven." (D&C 38:1; see also D&C 29:1; 39:1.) The Lord showed Abraham "the intelligences that were organized before the world was; [that] among all these there were many of the noble and great ones; and God saw these souls that they were good, and he stood in the midst of them, and he said: These I will make my rulers." (Abraham 3:22-23.) The Lord then revealed that Abraham was one of these intelligences, chosen and foreordained before he was born.

Scriptural verse continues: "There stood one among them that was like unto God, and he said unto those who were with him: We will go down . . . and we will make an earth whereon these may dwell." (Abraham 3:24.) Then "the Gods, organized and formed the heavens and the earth." (Abraham 4:1.) After the earth had been created, divided, beautified, and inhabited with plant and animal life, the crowning achievement of the creation was to be man — the human being. "So the Gods went down to organize man in their own image, . . . male and female, to form they them." (Abraham 4:27; see also Genesis 1:26-27.)

The very purpose of creation was to provide bodies, to

107

enable mortal life and experiences for these eagerly waiting spirits.

Question: What was the role of the priesthood in the process of creation?

The Prophet Joseph Smith taught: "The Priesthood is an everlasting principle, and existed with God from eternity.... Christ is the Great High Priest; Adam next.... The Priesthood was first given to Adam; he obtained the First Presidency, and held the keys of it from generation to generation. He obtained it in the Creation, before the world was formed." *(Teachings of the Prophet Joseph Smith*, pp. 157-58.)

President Brigham Young said, "Priesthood ... is the law by which the worlds are, were, and will continue for ever and ever." *(Discourses of Brigham Young*, 1966 ed., p. 130.)

Thus, priesthood is the power of God. Its ordinances and covenants are to bless men and women alike. By that power, the earth was created. Under the direction of the Father, Jehovah was the creator. As Michael, Adam did his part. He became the first man. But, in spite of the power and glory of creation to that point, the final link in the chain of creation was still missing. All the purposes of the world and all that was in the world would be brought to naught without woman—a keystone in the priesthood arch of creation.

When Eve was created—when her body was made by God—Adam exclaimed: "Bone of my bones, and flesh of my flesh; she shall be called Woman, because she was taken out of man." (Moses 3:23.)

Eve was formed from the rib of Adam. (See Genesis 2:22; Moses 3:22; Abraham 5:16.) Interesting to me is the fact that animals fashioned by our Creator, such as dogs and cats, have thirteen pairs of ribs, but the human being has one less with only twelve. I presume another bone could have been used, but the rib, coming as it does from the side, seems to denote partnership. The rib signifies neither dominion nor subservience, but a lateral relationship as partners, to work and to live, side by side.

Adam and Eve were joined together in marriage for time and for all eternity by the power of that everlasting priesthood. (See Genesis 2:24-25; Moses 3:24-25; Abraham 5:18-19.) Eve came as a partner, to build and to organize the bodies of mortal men. She was designed by Deity to co-create and nurture life, so that the great plan of the Father might achieve fruition. She was "the mother of all living" (Moses 4:26), the first of all women.

From our study of Eve, we may learn five fundamental lessons of everlasting importance:

1. Eve labored beside her companion, Adam. (See Moses 5:1.)

2. Eve and Adam bore the responsibilities of parenthood. (See Moses 5:2.)

3. Eve and Adam worshiped the Lord in prayer. (See Moses 5:4.)

4. Eve and Adam heeded divine commandments of obedience and sacrifice. (See Moses 5:5-6.)

5. Eve and Adam taught the gospel to their children. (See Moses 5:12.)

From these lessons we can study patterns that apply to present-day circumstances. Let us review them, lesson by lesson.

1. *Eve labored beside her companion.*

Adam held the priesthood, and Eve served in matriarchal partnership with the patriarchal priesthood. So today, each wife may join with her husband as a partner unified in purpose. Scriptures state clearly, "Neither is the man without the woman, neither the woman without the man, in the Lord." (1 Corinthians 11:11.) "They twain shall be one flesh." (Mark 10:8; D&C 49:16.)

Marvelously, it takes a man *and* a woman to make a man *or* a woman. Without union of the sexes, we can neither exist nor become perfect. Ordinary and imperfect people can build each other through their wholeness together. The complete contribution of one partner to the other is essential to exal-

109

THE POWER WITHIN US

tation. This is so in order that "the earth might answer the end of its creation." (D&C 49:16.)

So labor and love in partnership. Honor your companion. Any sense of competition for place or position is not appropriate for either partner, especially when enlightened by scriptural understanding.

2. *As Adam bore responsibilities of fatherhood, so Eve bore the responsibilities of motherhood.*

Eve did not shirk her responsibilities. To each sister, I say: With welcome arms you too may gratefully greet those children God may send, through your divine design as co-creator. With your husband, be obedient to the commandment to multiply and replenish the earth, as your opportunity, your spiritual guidance, your wisdom, and your health allow. You will gain joy and rejoicing in your posterity. That enrichment becomes more beautiful and precious with each passing year.

For those who are childless and those without companions, remember that the eternal timetable of the Lord is much longer than the lonely hours of your preparation or the totality of this mortal life. These are only as microseconds when compared to eternity. Your willingness and your worthiness are surely known to him. The spiritual rewards of motherhood are available to all women. Nurturing the young, comforting the frightened, protecting the vulnerable, teaching, and giving encouragement need not—indeed, should not—be limited to our own children.

Sisters, be patient. I know something of the pressures you feel. Your kitchens are too small. Your budgets are too tight. Demands upon you exceed your capacity to help all who cry out to you. Through it all, "improve the shining moments; don't let them pass you by." (*Hymns*, no. 226.) Take time for spiritual regeneration.

May I share a few lines by an unknown poet that have sustained Sister Nelson through the years. They also reflect her sense of priority:

Cleaning and scrubbing
Can wait till tomorrow,
For babies grow up,
We've learned to our sorrow.
So quiet down, cobwebs;
Dust, go to sleep.
I'm rocking my baby
And babies don't keep.

I'm glad Sister Nelson has not tried to be a "supermom." But she has been a "soothing" mom. This she has done simply by being herself. When priorities are in place, one can more patiently tolerate unfinished business.

"Time flies on wings of lightning; we cannot call it back." (*Hymns*, no. 226.) And while it passes, remember the precious eternal perspective. As you faithfully endure to the end, you will gain rewards promised by your Father in heaven. They include thrones, kingdoms, principalities, powers, dominions, glory, immortality, and eternal lives. (See D&C 75:5; 128:12-13; 132:19, 24; Moses 1:39.)

3. *Eve and her partner worshiped the Lord in prayer.*

As "Adam and Eve . . . called upon the name of the Lord" (Moses 5:4), a precedent was established. As each of us follows that pattern of prayer, blessings of wisdom and personal peace will ensue.

"Counsel with the Lord in all thy doings, and he will direct thee for good." (Alma 37:37.) Pray alone in your closet — in the solitude of your own sanctuary. Pour out the longings of your soul. Then pray with and for your husband, your sons and daughters, your sisters and brothers, your mother and father, and all in your family. Let the weight of your innocence be felt as you lovingly motivate others to good works. With your mind so attuned to the Lord and his power, your influence for good becomes immeasurably great. And in this world of sin and temptation, the power of prayer will protect you and be a shield for your loved ones.

I plead with the women of the Church to accept individual responsibility to know and to love the Lord. Communicate with

111

THE POWER WITHIN US

him. He will impress upon your mind inspiration and personal revelation to give you strength.

4. *Eve and her husband heeded divine commandments of obedience and sacrifice.*

Our first parents received "commandments that they should worship the Lord their God, and should offer ... an offering unto the Lord." (Moses 5:5.) They obeyed this direction to worship and sacrifice, and later they learned that this was "a similitude of the sacrifice of the Only Begotten of the Father, which is full of grace and truth." (Moses 5:7.)

When Christ came to the earth, he fulfilled the promised role as he became the ultimate sacrificial lamb. His atonement brought about a greater destiny and a nobler concept for us. We are still commanded to sacrifice, but not by shedding blood of animals.

Our highest sense of sacrifice is achieved as we make ourselves more sacred or holy. This we do by obedience to the commandments of God. Thus the laws of obedience and sacrifice are indelibly intertwined. Consider the commandments to obey the Word of Wisdom, to keep the Sabbath day holy, to pay an honest tithe. As we comply with these and other commandments, something wonderful happens to us. We become disciplined! We become disciples! We become more sacred and holy—more like our Lord!

I pay tribute to beloved ladies in my life who have taught sanctifying lessons to me. For a short time during the first year of our marriage, Sister Nelson maintained two jobs while I was in medical school. Before her paychecks had arrived, we found ourselves owing more than our funds could defray, so we took advantage of an option then available to sell blood at twenty-five dollars a pint. In an interval between her daytime job as a schoolteacher and her evening work as a clerk in a music store, we went to the hospital and each sold a pint of blood. As the needle was withdrawn from her arm, she said to me, "Don't forget to pay tithing on my blood money." (When her mother learned I was bleeding her daughter between two jobs,

I sensed at that time she may not have been too pleased with her new son-in-law.) Such obedience was a tremendous lesson to me. Sister Nelson's commitment to tithe became my commitment too.

You righteous daughters, never underestimate the influence for good you can exert upon your fathers. I haven't met a father yet who claimed to be perfect. So in his imperfection, stand steadfast in loving patience with your dad. Let me illustrate this point with a personal story.

Many years ago when our daughters were very young, Sister Nelson and I took them fishing. We were having a wonderful time. Everyone was catching fish. Then shades of Saturday night's darkness brought a curfew to our fun. So great was my enthusiasm for our success that I allowed myself to rationalize aloud with the girls. (Rationalization is one of the real obstacles to obedience.) Knowing that the next day was Sunday, I jokingly said, "If we get up tomorrow two hours earlier than normal, we can catch some more fish and then quit promptly at our usual wake-up hour."

Silence followed. My companion and our daughters glared at me. Icy stillness was broken when our seven-year-old said: "Daddy, would you eat those fish you caught on Sunday?" Then she added: "Would you ask Heavenly Father to bless fish you caught on the Sabbath?"

Needless to say, we did no fishing the next morning. My family's commitment to the Sabbath became my commitment, too.

As you obey each of God's commandments, your holiness will fortify the foundation of your father's faith. When the two of you are together spiritually, one plus one is clearly greater than two.

5. *Adam and Eve taught the gospel to their children.*

Today, men and women still have that worthy work to do. But before you can teach, you must first learn of your premortal existence, the creation, the fall, the atonement of Christ, and the reason for mortality. Study the scriptures and internalize

113

them. Teach faith, repentance, baptism, and the gift of the Holy Ghost. Then let your commitment to the mission of the Church be evident in all you do. Preaching the gospel, perfecting the Saints, and redeeming members of your family will cause you to concentrate on covenants and ordinances of eternal significance.

As you exercise your agency, teach things that are elevating and useful. Teach the principles of honesty, self-reliance, avoidance of unnecessary debt. You will build a more stable society by so doing. And remember your example. What you are is more important than what you do or what you say.

No one can do all things. Circumstances, available time, and talents vary widely. As your diversity takes you to various arenas of activity, let your presence be felt.

Your foes in a sordid society demean the sacredness of women and the sanctity of motherhood. Your world, sickened by unchastity and plagued with sexually transmitted disease, needs your righteous example. The wrath of God is provoked by governments that sponsor gambling, condone pornography, or legalize abortion. These forces serve to denigrate women now, just as they did in the days of Sodom and Gomorrah.

You can—you must—make a difference. You are vital to the Lord's team—one team, with one purpose. Through their diversity, our sisters can build strength in unity and bind themselves together in all holiness. Anchor yourself to "the foundation of the apostles and prophets, Jesus Christ himself being the chief corner stone." (Ephesians 2:20.)

Let us heed this teaching from the Book of Mormon: "Remember that it is upon the rock of our Redeemer, who is Christ, the Son of God, that ye must build your foundation; that when the devil shall send forth his mighty winds, yea, his shafts in the whirlwind, yea, when all his hail and his mighty storm shall beat upon you, it shall have no power over you to drag you down to the gulf of misery and endless wo, because of the rock upon which ye are built, which is a sure foundation, a foundation whereon if men build they cannot fall." (Helaman 5:12.)

May we all let our lives be committed to our Father in heaven, to his Only Begotten Son, and to his church restored by them in this latter day. A dispensation of the gospel has been entrusted to our care. Everlasting priesthood principles, laws, and powers depend upon our partnership.

Chapter 13

FORCES IN LIFE: A DADDY-DAUGHTER DIALOGUE

It was one of those memorable moments—one of those special times when a wonderful daughter comes to her loving father with an honest question that deserves a careful answer. The question of this attractive teenage daughter was "How far can I go with boys and still maintain acceptable standards with you and with my Father in heaven?"

Sensing the opportunity to teach a vital lesson, the father philosophically replied, "There are two important forces in the world—centrifugal forces and centripetal forces. The term *centrifugal* force comes from Latin roots meaning 'fleeing from the center.' *Centripetal* force is 'a force directed toward the center.' "

"Oh, Dad!" she interrupted. "I ask a simple question and you give me a complicated answer! Can't you just give me a simple answer?"

"What was your question again?"

"The question, Dad, was 'Just how far can I go and still be proper?' "

"Well, my dear daughter, it all depends on where you want to go," the father answered as he gently led her by the arm over to her mother's nearby quilting project. "Let's take a little tuft of this cotton upstairs to your room and put it on the turntable of your record player." He molded the cotton into a small ball with his fingers as they entered her room and walked over to the record player. Then he placed the ball on the very edge of the turntable and said, "Now turn it on."

She did so, and after three or four revolutions the little cotton ball went flying out into the room.

"Turn the record player off," the father directed, "and put the cotton at the center of the disk. Now turn it on again."

She did as she was told, and around and around the turntable went. But this time the tuft of cotton did not move.

"That is what I mean by centrifugal and centripetal forces," the father continued. "One force causes an object to flee from the center, and the other directs an object toward the center."

He smiled as he reminded his daughter of one of her favorite rides at the amusement park when she was younger. "Remember how much time you used to spend on that large spinning turntable in the fun house, and how you and all the other children would scramble toward the center and try to hold your places as the huge wheel spun?"

"Oh, yes," the daughter replied. "Once that wheel started spinning, the kids closest to the edge went sliding off just like that cotton ball, and the ones who managed to hold their position near the center stayed on."

Her eyes sparkled as she remembered how she would slip and slide on the big wheel. "I tried my best to work my way from the edge toward the center, but it was a real struggle. I had to crawl and apply great traction with my hands to pull myself up toward the center. And if that weren't hard enough, I always had to be on guard for those who didn't make it, because they usually grabbed someone else as they spun off and tried to take the other person with them."

"In a way, life is like that," her father explained. "There are struggles, and people going downward sometimes tend to drag those nearby down with them. We, on the other hand, are trying to climb against those forces that are pulling us down.

"Now back to your question. How far you can go as you enjoy the companionship of your friends depends on where you want to go. If you want to go up and onward, you behave one way. If you want to go down and out, you behave another way."

"I want to go up, Dad," she replied without hesitation. "I want to reach my goals."

Since his daughter had recently attended a lecture by a member of a team that tried to conquer Mount Everest, the father could not resist another comparison. "If that's the direction you want to go, let's take some lessons from those expert mountain climbers you met. What do you remember most about their experiences?"

"Oh, I learned a lot, but the most important thing I remember is their advance planning. They anticipated everything that could possibly happen and were prepared with decisions made well in advance in response to whatever they might encounter.

"Their teamwork was really impressive to me too. Since they had tremendous hardships to overcome and heights to climb, they linked themselves together with ropes. The ropes were attached to something solid above so they could pull themselves up. Occasionally even the other people to whom they were linked became their anchors. We saw photographs showing a person dangling in midair while being tethered to people he trusted both above and below. Yet he didn't fall because of his ties to other people.

"The people also maintained excellent communication. Even though they might have been temporarily separated, they were always in good communication. It seemed that the closer they were to potential danger, the more they leaned toward the center."

After hearing his daughter's report, the father responded, "Did anyone ever ask the question 'How close to the edge can I come?' No! Quite to the contrary. Their emphasis always seemed to be 'How close to the center can I stay?' "

Then, with a look of enlightenment, she replied, "Dad, now I am beginning to understand."

The father continued, "Let's apply these lessons to your question. One of the most important things you can do as you face the challenging climb of life is to plan in advance. You must know what pitfalls might befall you. No matter what your problem may be, you must decide in advance how you will react, what actions you will take, just like the mountain climbers on Mount Everest.

"Remember that you are part of a team that is pulling for you. You are connected by unseen tethers of love to people who pray and pull for you daily, even though those ties are not as visible as the ropes of the mountain climbers. Your teammates even extend into the world beyond. Every one of your ancestors, both those living and those who have passed on to the other side, is concerned about you and supporting you. Relatives, teachers in school and in church, and good friends always try to lift. If you ever have acquaintances who are trying to pull you with them on their downward drift, know that those people are not truly your friends at all. Real friends never pull you down; they always lift.

"Communication in your life is as important to you as it is for mountain climbers. That's why I think you are so special for wanting to communicate with your father when you have such an important question. Just as receptive as your earthly father is your Heavenly Father, who appreciates your communications with him in prayer.

"Finally, when dangers do come, always look toward the center. Remember, your record player would not produce very good music if it were not for that rod in the center that anchors the record to the spinning disk. If you allow the world in which your activities revolve to be anchored centrally to the iron rod of the gospel, life's music will be sweet for you.

"On this or any other important question you have, cling to the center. Know what your loved ones would do in a similar circumstance. Think what the Lord would counsel you to do.

If you are firmly and securely anchored to the iron rod, which is the word of God, you'll be safe in your activities. The wiles of your whirling world and the winds of temptation will not spin you off, but will find you safely rooted *centrally* toward your quest for salvation and exaltation.

"God has great blessings in store for you. You will attain the heights that he has placed within your grasp. Ultimately he will reward you through your obedience. Listen to his promise: If you are faithful, you 'shall inherit thrones, kingdoms, principalities, and powers, dominions, . . . and a continuation of the seeds forever and ever.' [D&C 132:19.] This, my daughter, is what I want for you."

The lovely daughter thanked her father with a warm hug, grateful for his love and understanding. She now knew that she was no longer interested in the answer to her question. She didn't want to know how close to the edge she could go. She was determined now to stay close to the center, where the great rewards of fulfillment in life are found.

Chapter 14

TEN COMMANDMENTS

Our turn on earth is so new—so exciting—so full of adventure. Sometimes it is difficult for us to realize that the world is pretty old and that the challenges we face are old too. We are newcomers on a very old stage. The plot of the drama is already well written. We enter, prepare for performance, and then brace ourselves for the final curtain call. Our turn on the stage of life's theater is now—a special and an exciting opportunity.

A monument in Chicago bears an inscription with a message something like this: "Time flies, you say? Alas, I know. It's Time that stays. It's only we who go."

Each of us enters the scene of mortality for a brief season. We are born. We grow. We encounter tests and trials. We win a few, lose a few, and then we pass on. We came to earth for two reasons: to get a body and to develop faith, which is sometimes best measured as the power of the spirit over the appetites of the body.

The bodies we came to receive have many physical appetites—for food, for drink, for exercise of all living systems. We like to see, hear, smell, touch, and taste. We hunger, we thirst, we crave affection, approval, and attention. These appetites are God-given—for our survival, for our protection, and for our joy.

In satisfying these appetites, we make choices. For example, on New Year's Eve, we may indulge in chips and dip, candy and cake, drink and doughnuts, and derive deserved discomfort. On New Year's morn, we resolve to make better selections and be wiser next time.

Our more important choices are those between right and wrong. Inasmuch as good and evil forces do exist in the world, it is not surprising that they compete most keenly in the arena of appetite—yes, in each of our many physical appetites. Many choices have moral implications. There are good and there are evil things that we may see. There are good and there are evil things that we may listen to. There are good and there are evil things that we may feel, eat, drink, or otherwise allow into our bodies. I would define *moral* in terms of commandments of God. Something is moral if it is in line with direction he has given. Something is immoral if it conflicts with his will.

It is important to know who we are, why we are here, and where we want to go. We must remember that we are sons and daughters of God. He created us; we did not create ourselves. And he didn't leave us alone. As a loving Creator, he gave us a book of instructions. We call that book *scripture*. We pluralize the word and call it *scriptures* because his commandments have been recorded in different volumes, many times and in many places. But the message of morality has always been the same.

The Ten Commandments comprise the great moral code of our society. They have been repeated over and over again. They were cited more than once in the Old Testament (see Exodus 20; Deuteronomy 5), reiterated in the New Testament (see Romans 13:9), written in the Book of Mormon (see Mosiah 13:12-24), and recorded in the Doctrine and Covenants (see D&C 42:18-28). We had better memorize them, just as we have learned the alphabet and multiplication tables.

The first four commandments pertain to our relationship with God, the remaining six to our relationships with fellow human beings. As we consider each of them, we might reflect not only on God the Giver, but also on Satan the opposer. All good in the world comes from God; all evil stems from Satan. As the evil one, Satan fights against each commandment and creates conflict in the minds of mortals on each of the ten. He further hopes that conflicting thoughts will be followed by deeds counter to divine commandments, thereby enslaving our souls and denying us blessings from heaven.

Our Creator identified himself before giving the Ten Commandments, so that there would be no question as to who was speaking. "I am the Lord thy God," he began.

1. *"Thou shalt have no other gods before me."* (Exodus 20:2-3.)

This means that before we strive for dollars or degrees, power or position, our individual system of priority puts him where he belongs, as our loving Father—right on the top of our list. I hope you personally pray to him each day. " 'Ere you left your room this morning, did you think to pray?" (*Hymns,* no. 140.) If you didn't, repent! Fathers love to hear from their children, morning and night. Our Heavenly Father is no exception.

2. *"Thou shalt not make unto thee any graven image . . . [and] bow down thyself to them."* (Exodus 20:4-5.)

The children of Israel, to whom this commandment was originally given, had been making colossal statues of Pharaoh. So imbued were they with such practices that, when left on their own, they fashioned a golden calf and presumed to worship it.

Is this commandment still relevant in our day? It most certainly is. In one country I visited recently, for example, people kneel in worship before an object of their own creation. It has the body of a man and the head of an elephant. They call him Lord (Ganesh) and pray to him. In fact, in many of the most populous and poverty-stricken nations of the earth, images and statuary constitute the object of adoration of people in ignorance of this great second commandment. Their disobedience keeps them from the blessings of prosperity that God has promised to his faithful children.

3. *"Thou shalt not take the name of the Lord thy God in*

vain; for the Lord will not hold him guiltless that taketh his name in vain." (Exodus 20:7.)

The lips and tongue are among the many important organs in the body. Just as they play a role in tasting various foods and drinks we choose to take into our bodies, so they also communicate what we choose to give out from our bodies. Swearing and profanity are darkness in the language of the undisciplined. Such are symbols of the unlearned and evidences of a mind without better vocabulary.

Let us not offend people by unkind language and, most important of all, let us not separate ourselves from the love of God by taking his name in vain. I like these verses from Proverbs: "I will speak of excellent things; and the opening of my lips shall be right things. For my mouth shall speak truth; and wickedness is an abomination to my lips. All the words of my mouth are in righteousness; there is nothing . . . perverse in them." (Proverbs 8:6-8.)

4. *"Remember the sabbath day, to keep it holy."* (Exodus 20:8.)

In taking this commandment seriously, the early children of Israel compiled long lists of deeds that were not permitted on the Sabbath. The Savior came later to clarify that man was not created for the Sabbath, but the Sabbath was created for man. (See Mark 2:27.)

When I was a youth, I wondered just what activities were appropriate for the Sabbath. I read lists of dos and don'ts, all prepared by others. But now I have a much better understanding. I gained precious insight from two Old Testament scriptures. The first is from Exodus: "The Lord spake unto Moses, saying, . . . My sabbaths ye shall keep: for it is a sign between me and you throughout your generations; that ye may know that I am the Lord that doth sanctify you." (Exodus 31:12-13.) The other scripture is from Ezekiel: "I gave them my sabbaths, to be a sign between me and them, that they might know that I am the Lord that sanctify them. . . . I am the Lord your God; . . . hallow my sabbaths; and they shall be a sign between

me and you, that ye may know that I am the Lord your Gc
(Ezekiel 20:12, 19-20.)

Now I understand that my behavior on the Sabbath is my
sign to the Lord of my regard for him and for the covenant
under which I was born. If, on the one hand, my interests on
the Sabbath were turned to pro football games or worldly
movies, the sign from me to him would clearly be that my
devotion would *not* favor the Lord. If, on the other hand, my
Sabbath interests were focused on the Lord and his teachings,
my family, or the sick, or the poor, and the needy, that sign
would likewise be visible to God. Our activities on the Sabbath
will be appropriate as we consider them to be our personal
sign to him of our commitment to the Lord.

5. *"Honour thy father and thy mother: that thy days may
be long upon the land which the Lord thy God giveth thee."*
(Exodus 20:12.)

This is the first commandment listed with a promise. And
you need to remember that sometimes parents may not fully
understand why they counsel as they do.

May I relate a story to illustrate? Several years ago, I was
commissioned to give an important lecture at a university in
New York City. The night before the lecture, Sister Nelson and
I were invited to dinner at the home of our host professor.
During the course of the evening, he proudly introduced us
to his beautiful twenty-one-year-old daughter, an honor student
in medical school and an unusually attractive, gifted, and bril-
liant person. The next day, I gave my lecture, and we returned
to our home with pleasant memories.

Some weeks later, the professor, in an obvious state of
grief, called me on the telephone in Salt Lake City. I asked,
"What is the matter?"

"Remember my daughter whom you met at our home?"

"Of course," I replied. "I'll never forget such a stunning
young woman."

"Last night she was killed in an automobile accident! My

wife and I are inconsolably beside ourselves. We needed to talk to someone, so we called you."

"Tell me about it," I said.

Then he related the circumstances. "Last night she asked permission to go to a dance with a certain young man. I didn't have a good feeling about it. I told her so and asked her not to go. She asked me why I felt that way. I simply told her that I was uneasy. Ours has been a close family, and she had always been an obedient daughter, but this time she said that if I couldn't give her a good reason to decline, she wanted to go. And so she did. At the dance, alcoholic beverages were served. Her escort drank a bit—we don't know how much. While returning home, he was driving too fast—missed a turn—and careened his car through a guardrail and into a reservoir below. They were both submerged and taken to their death."

I tried to interject my feeling of shared sadness, but he continued. "My grief is made worse because I had the distinct feeling before she left that trouble lay ahead. Why couldn't I have been more persuasive? If I had been more insistent, she would be alive today, and her pure life—so full of promise— would still be ahead of her. Now it is all over, and I have myself to blame."

Meanwhile, on my end of the phone, I felt helpless. But in the back of my mind, and as a father of nine lovely daughters, the message flashed across my mind: "Honour thy father and thy mother: that thy days may be long upon the land which the Lord thy God giveth thee."

Parents are entitled to receive heavenly promptings for the protection of their children. Sometimes they can't explain good reasons for counsel they give. Inspiration is sometimes difficult to describe, but it is just as real as is communication from the spoken or written word.

Threats to a person's longevity and happiness may come in various forms. The harmful effects of tobacco, alcohol, tea, and coffee are widely known. Parents advise against their use because our Heavenly Father has forbidden them. (See D&C

89.) Drug abuse is another danger. Pushers of drugs may invade campuses or convenience stores, cunningly posing as friends. They would entice youth through appetites of the flesh to take into their bodies substances that would alter the mind. Addictions of the flesh become addictions of the spirit as well. Young people need to keep their minds and their bodies free from pollution and from bondage. They will be free, live longer, and be happier if they will so protect themselves.

6. *"Thou shalt not kill."* (Exodus 20:13.)

Simple words — and not much temptation to break this commandment, you may add. But to clarify, in our day the Lord added, "Thou shalt not . . . kill, nor do anything like unto it." (D&C 59:6.) Do you think he could foresee our time, when mankind would disregard reverence for life and authorize abortion on a massive scale throughout the world? Of course he could. That is why he warned us again. Few acts could bring guilt and sorrow quite so surely as the shedding of innocent blood, regardless of the age of the victim. We need this counsel today, perhaps more than ever before.

7. *"Thou shalt not commit adultery."* (Exodus 20:14.)

Our Creator knew that our appetites for affection could escape control, so he protected us by giving this commandment. We may think we live in a more permissive society today than did people of former times, but I think it's only because we are actors on the stage of today.

A search of the scriptures teaches us important lessons on this subject. The word *adultery* — or its derivatives — appears in 113 verses of scripture. One-third of those references appear in the Old Testament, one-third in the New Testament, and one-third in scripture brought forth in modern day.

Adultery's companion sin, fornication, is also forbidden by the Lord. This word — or its derivatives — appears in the scriptures in 54 verses, again spanning all time. Nearly three-quarters of those references appear in the New Testament; 9 percent are in the Old Testament; and the remaining 17 percent are in the books of the triple combination.

These commandments against sexual sin are not from parents, teachers, school boards, doctors, or any mere mortal. They are from God our Maker — and the punishments of God will be delivered upon those who transgress. Transgressors will be accountable directly to him. The Lord said, "Every man may act in doctrine and principle . . . according to the moral agency which I have given unto him, that every man may be accountable for his own sins in the day of judgment." (D&C 101:78.)

When Jesus lived upon the earth, he taught a higher law, one limited not just to deed but to thought as well. He said, "Whosoever looketh on a woman to lust after her hath committed adultery with her already in his heart." (Matthew 5:28.) He was telling us not even to look at forbidden offerings that might tempt us at the table of sexual appetite.

Today, people are appropriately fearful of Acquired Immune Deficiency Syndrome, or AIDS. Generally, it is a sexually transmitted condition, most commonly encountered among those engaging in homosexual activity. Public health authorities forecast that within our lifetime, AIDS will become a plague that will sweep the earth unlike any other experienced in modern times.

Some have wondered, Is this a way the Lord has of punishing those who transgress the law of chastity, which forbids sexual relations outside the covenant of marriage? I don't know. But I do know of scriptural illustrations of the Lord destroying the wicked.

Why did the flood come at the time of Noah? Why did the Lord destroy Sodom and Gomorrah? Remember the interesting dialogue between the Lord and Abraham, who asked if these two cities could be spared if fifty righteous inhabitants could be found? The Lord agreed. Then Abraham engaged in an interesting exercise. He seemed to bargain with the Lord, inquiring, "How about forty-five righteous?" When he received a stay of destruction with that number, he plied the Lord with successive questions of forty, thirty, twenty, or ten righteous.

The Lord even agreed to spare them — if ten righteous could be identified. But the cities of Sodom and Gomorrah were destroyed, for the Lord rained down fire and brimstone upon them.

Another instance of guilt and punishment is recorded in First Chronicles, wherein David said to God, "I have sinned greatly," and then submitted himself for discipline. The Lord offered three choices, one of which David was required to make: either three years of famine, or three months to be destroyed by his foes, or three days of pestilence in the land, wherein the angel of the Lord would work destruction throughout all the coasts of Israel.

David made an interesting choice. He preferred not to fall into the hands of man, but to be dealt with by the Lord himself. He selected option number three. "So the Lord sent pestilence upon Israel: and there fell of Israel seventy thousand men." (See 1 Chronicles 21:1-14.)

Elijah prophesied that the people in his day would be destroyed because they walked in the way of sexual sin: "Behold, with a great plague will the Lord smite thy people, and thy children, and thy wives, and all thy goods." (2 Chronicles 21:13-14.)

Another reference involves the city of Capernaum, now but a desolate ruin of a once thriving community. Jesus said, "Capernaum, which art exalted unto heaven, shalt be brought down to hell: for if the mighty works, which have been done in thee, had been done in Sodom, it would have remained until this day. But I say unto you, That it shall be more tolerable for the land of Sodom in the day of judgment, than for thee." (Matthew 11:23-24.) So Capernaum, too, was cursed because of the iniquities of its people. Today it lies in ruin, silently signaling the power of God to bless or to punish, according to the faith of the people.

No, I don't think plague, punishment, and retribution upon the wicked are new. They are as old as the law that forbids sexual relations outside the covenant of marriage, either between the sexes or among the sexes.

One of the many tragedies of sin is that wickedness of the sinner may inflict misery upon innocent victims as well. Just as it occurs in war, so it can also occur with AIDS, when blameless marriage partners or clean children may become afflicted with the virus initially acquired through someone else's transgression.

That doesn't seem right, you say? No, it doesn't. But one thing is right: Each of us will be judged by the Lord when life on earth is completed. His judgment will be right; it will be merciful and just, and our eternal existence will be determined in accordance with our personal thoughts, deeds, and faith, and not by those of any other. As we protect ourselves by obedience to the law of chastity, we will be blessed by the Lord, now and forever more.

8. *"Thou shalt not steal."* (Exodus 20:15.)

This commandment teaches us to honor others and reverence that which is rightfully theirs. The qualities of honesty, integrity, dependability, and trust are personal characteristics that are more valuable than material wealth.

A person who keeps this commandment does not accept the philosophy of obtaining something for nothing. The true follower of Christ pays for services rendered or goods received, and likewise renders service or goods in return for compensation received. This is an important reason why we oppose governmentally sponsored lotteries. For the few winners, there are losers — manyfold — and no one receives remuneration that was earned. As Elder Dallin H. Oaks recently stated, "That governments would tolerate gambling is regrettable; that governments would promote gambling is reprehensible." ("Gambling—Morally Wrong and Politically Unwise," *Ensign*, June 1987, p. 75.)

We must be certain our own consciences are free from guilt. We must not rob or steal or shoplift or "anything like unto it." We can be protected from the disease of greed, which seems to underlie these problems, through the divine commandment of tithing. It gives great security. If a person learns to be honest in financial dealings with God, that individual is likely to be honest elsewhere, and success in life will ensue.

As we are reminded of the Lord's commandment for tithing, think of your own compliance with this eighth commandment: "Will a man rob God? Yet ye have robbed me. But ye say, Wherein have we robbed thee? In tithes and offerings. . . . Bring ye all the tithes into the storehouse . . . and prove me now herewith, saith the Lord of hosts, if I will not open you the windows of heaven, and pour you out a blessing, that there shall not be room enough to receive it." (Malachi 3:8, 10.) The law of tithing is a valuable key to the blessings of honesty and prosperity.

9. *"Thou shalt not bear false witness against thy neighbour."* (Exodus 20:16.)

Nothing is more precious to an individual than his good name. Following the Civil War, a certain financial institution invited General Robert E. Lee to be its president at a handsome salary. The officers of the company explained that they didn't care about his service. They said, "What we want is your name." The great general replied, "Gentlemen, my name is not for sale."

Shakespeare wrote:

> Who steals my purse steals trash. . . .
> But he who filches from me my good name
> Robs me of that which not enriches him
> And makes me poor indeed.
> (*Othello*, Act III, scene 3.)

Let us oft speak kind words to each other and about each other, and, in truth, always be obedient to the ninth commandment.

10. *"Thou shalt not covet."* (Exodus 20:17.)

To this great directive, the Lord singled out, in addition, "thy neighbour's wife" and maidservant or manservant. This commandment reinforces commandment number seven, which forbids adultery. Knowing of our potential weaknesses, the Lord repeated the need for moral purity in at least two of the ten commandments, and did so to people of Old Testament, New Testament, and Book of Mormon times, as well as to us in our day. While society and governments grapple with problems of teenage pregnancy, abortion, sexually transmitted disease, and all the social ills associated with each, the teachings of our Creator ring loud and clear. They are as true now as they have ever been. They are as essential to happiness now as they were when first given. From Sinai's Mount, the Lord God thundered down these commandments, and he has repeated them over and over again to successive generations. Each person must develop the power of the spirit to be stronger than the appetites of the body.

Great rewards are promised. Instead of being tossed scraps with the taste of a crumb here or a morsel there, if we are obedient to the Lord's commandments we may feast continually at the banquet table of life. As our physical appetites and passions are controlled and these commandments are obeyed, incredible blessings will be ours. We will be healthier. We will be happier. We will find wisdom, even hidden treasures of knowledge. We will prosper in the land. And even more: To those who are faithful, he has promised that we shall inherit thrones, kingdoms, principalities, and powers, dominions, exaltation, glory, and eternal lives. (See D&C 132:19.)

Chapter 15

COVENANTS AND SIGNS

Isaiah 42:6 states: "I the Lord have called thee in righteousness, and will hold thine hand, and will keep thee, and give thee for a covenant of the people, for a light of the Gentiles." Again, in our day the Lord identified his everlasting covenant as a light to the world: "I have sent mine everlasting covenant into the world, to be a light to the world, and to be a standard for my people." (D&C 45:9.)

Scriptures reveal that our Heavenly Father has often used tokens or signs to guide and teach his people pertaining to covenants in his eternal plan for us. Often, references to these are repeated, even in different books of scripture. I would like to comment on ten of these unique events of scriptural history, past, present, and future, that link a covenant to a token or sign.

1. THE RAINBOW

Covenant number one pertains to Noah, Enoch, the flood, and the rainbow: "I establish my covenant with you, and with your seed after you; . . . neither shall there any more be a flood to destroy the earth. And God said, This [rainbow] is the token of the covenant which I make between me and you and every living creature that is with you, for perpetual generations: I do set my bow in the cloud, and it shall be for a token of a covenant between me and the earth. . . . And God said unto Noah, This is the token of the covenant, which I have established between me and all flesh that is upon the earth." (Genesis 9:9-11, 17.)

135

Later revelation enlarges the terms of this covenant, that the Zion of Enoch will return and the Lord will come again to dwell on earth. (See JST, Genesis 9:17-25.)

The token of the rainbow is a visible and perpetual reminder of the three terms of this covenant.

2. CIRCUMCISION

The second covenant is known as the Abrahamic covenant. Note the words of God to father Abraham: "Thou shalt keep my covenant . . . thou, and thy seed after thee in their generations. This is my covenant, . . . Every man child among you shall be circumcised . . . and it shall be a token of the covenant betwixt me and you." (Genesis 17:9-11.)

Abraham first received the gospel by baptism (the covenant of salvation). Then the higher priesthood was conferred upon him, and he entered into celestial marriage (the covenant of exaltation). Finally he received a promise that these blessings would be offered to all of his mortal posterity. Included in the divine promises to Abraham were assurances that Christ would come through his lineage, that Abraham's posterity would receive certain lands as an eternal inheritance, that all nations of the earth would be blessed by his seed, and more. Since we are descendants of Abraham, Isaac, and Jacob, generally through Joseph, we inherit these blessings. Those who are faithful to covenants made in the house of the Lord will receive an inheritance in the celestial kingdom.

Christ later revealed, "The [token] of circumcision is done away in me." (Moroni 8:8.) Latter-day revelation also confirms that this law was fulfilled in Christ. (See D&C 74:3-7.) But the Abrahamic covenant remains!

3. PASSOVER

Covenant number three pertains to the Passover. These are the words of the Lord: "The blood . . . on the two side posts and on the upper door post . . . shall be . . . for a token upon the houses where ye are: and when I see the blood, I will pass over you, and the plague shall not be upon you to destroy you, when I smite the land of Egypt." (Exodus 12:7, 13.)

The covenant of the Passover included a token rendered in faith, which spared the lives of firstborn sons.

4. SABBATH DAY

Covenant number four pertains to the Sabbath day. For years we have been taught to keep the Sabbath day holy and have struggled for understanding and compliance with this law. Keeping the Sabbath day holy is a sign of a covenant with the Lord. He decreed: "Verily my sabbaths ye shall keep: for it is a sign between me and you throughout your generations; that ye may know that I am the Lord that doth sanctify you." (Exodus 31:13.)

That expression from Exodus was reiterated by the Lord through Ezekiel, who said, "Hallow my sabbaths; and they shall be a sign between me and you, that ye may know that I am the Lord your God." (Ezekiel 20:20.)

As I worked among the people of mainland China, I noted that their calendars, like ours, distinguish Sundays in red numerals while those for the other six days of the week are printed in black. On Sunday the shops are generally closed, and only emergency operations are performed in the hospitals. When I asked my medical associates why they regarded Sunday different from other days, they replied, "Because we have learned from Western culture that people seem to be more productive if they take Sunday off." When I asked if there were any religious significance to their special treatment of Sunday, my hosts indicated that they were not aware of any. What a glorious day it will be when these wonderful people are blessed for keeping the Sabbath day holy for the right reason. It is man's sign to God acknowledging that He is the Lord.

5. CROSSING OF THE JORDAN

Covenant number five pertains to the Israelites, who crossed the waters of the Jordan when Joshua led them into that swollen river at flood time. They had complete faith that God would "heap up" the waters of the river Jordan as he had done earlier when the Red Sea was parted for Moses and his followers. After the people had successfully accomplished this act of faith, facilitated by a miracle from the Lord, they were commanded that a man from each tribe take a stone and erect a monument to signify this event. Joshua set up twelve stones in the place where the priests stood responding to the Lord's directive "that this may be a sign among you" (Joshua 4:6) — a sign of their covenant with the Lord, who delivered them in safety to their destination.

6. BIRTH OF JESUS

The sixth covenant pertains to the birth of Jesus Christ. Remember the prophecy of Isaiah often quoted at Christmastime: "Behold, a virgin shall conceive, and bear a son, and shall call his name Immanuel." Immediately preceding those words is this significant preamble: "The Lord himself shall give you a sign." (Isaiah 7:14; 2 Nephi 17:14.)

The Christmas message also contains this familiar passage: "For unto you is born this day in the city of David a Saviour, which is Christ the Lord. And this shall be a sign unto you; Ye shall find the babe wrapped in swaddling clothes, lying in a manger." (Luke 2:11-12.) The birth of the Son of God was a covenant made from before the foundation of the world. It had other celestial signs: "I give unto you . . . a sign at the time of his coming; for behold, there shall be great lights in heaven, insomuch that in the night before he cometh there shall be no darkness. . . . There shall a new star arise, . . . and this also shall be a sign unto you." (Helaman 14:3, 5; see also 3 Nephi 1:21-22.)

This wondrous event was heralded by wondrous signs given to both the old world and the new.

7. THE DEATH OF JESUS

Covenant number seven is the atoning sacrifice and crucifixion of Jesus Christ. The most important event ever to occur

138

in the history of this world was commemorated by heavenly signs. A prophet foretold a sign of his death: "The sun shall be darkened and refuse to give his light unto you; and also the moon and the stars; and there shall be no light upon the face of this land . . . for the space of three days, to the time that he shall rise again from the dead." (Helaman 14:20.) Eyewitness accounts of the awesome reality of those signs were recorded in other verses of scripture. (3 Nephi 8:3; 11:2.)

These seven covenants, tokens, and signs are all past history. The next three pertain to our day and to the future.

8. THOSE WHO WOULD DECEIVE

Covenant number eight pertains to falsehood. When the Savior was asked, "What shall be the sign of thy [second] coming?," he listed many signs. But the first one he mentioned was "Take heed that no man deceive you." (Matthew 24:3-4; JS–Matthew 1:5.) Then he warned that false prophets shall rise, and shall deceive many, and that, "if possible, they shall deceive the very elect, who are the elect according to the covenant." (JS–Matthew 1:22; emphasis added.) That means that each of us, the elect of the Lord — the elect according to the covenant — will be subject to deceit and deception by those who would divert us from our commitment to follow the Savior. This word of warning hopefully is sufficient to the wise.

9. THE EVERLASTING COVENANT

Covenant number nine: Each member of the Church is under covenant to walk in accordance with the commandments of God. Modern scripture reveals tokens that pertain to this covenant. Have you ever wondered why we kneel in prayer? Scripture answers: "Let him offer himself in prayer upon his knees before God, in token or remembrance of the everlasting covenant." (D&C 88:131.) The everlasting covenant is the gospel of Jesus Christ. (See D&C 66:2.)

Scripture affirms that the amen we offer at the close of a prayer is also a token of the everlasting covenant. When we audibly say "amen" at the conclusion of the remarks of one who has spoken, it may be regarded as a token of an eternal covenant. (See D&C 88:135.)

10. THE LAST DAYS

The tenth covenant is a multifaceted one, pertaining to the events of the last days and the great millennial reign of the Lord. Did you know the Book of Mormon is a sign of that covenant? The heading to chapter 29 of Third Nephi states: "The coming forth of the Book of Mormon is a sign that the Lord has commenced to gather Israel and fulfill his covenants."

News media have carried stories occasionally of incidents pertaining to the early history of the Church and the coming forth of the Book of Mormon. What these news accounts fail to report is that the Book of Mormon has come forth in fulfillment of prophecy, ancient and modern, and that it was translated by the gift and power of God, then pronounced as the most nearly correct book on the face of the earth. Reporters may also fail to note that it is a sign of the covenant of God to the world that the last days are forthcoming. We will be accountable not to news reports, but to this scripture: "Ye need not suppose that ye can turn the right hand of the Lord unto the left, that he may not execute judgment unto the fulfilling of the covenant which he hath made unto the house of Israel." (3 Nephi 29:9.)

The Lord listed other signs of his covenant to come again: "Ye shall hear of wars and rumours of wars. . . . There shall be famines, and pestilences, and earthquakes. . . . Iniquity shall abound, the love of many shall wax cold. . . . This gospel of the kingdom shall be preached in all the world for a witness unto all nations; and then shall the end come." (Matthew 24:6-14.)

To the people on the American continent, the Lord added, "I give unto you a sign . . . that I shall gather in, from their long dispersion, my people, O house of Israel. . . . This is the thing which I will give unto you for a sign . . . that the covenant of the Father may be fulfilled which he hath covenanted with his people, O house of Israel." (3 Nephi 21:1-4.) In that day there will be a marvelous work among the people. The lost tribes will return and the new Jerusalem will be built.

As a final prelude to the covenant of his coming, other signs will be seen: the sun will be darkened, the moon will be darkened, and stars will fall from heaven. (See Matthew 24:29-30; D&C 88:87, 93; JS–Matthew 1:33.)

We are a covenant people. Signs and tokens of God's covenants with us are all around. We have just reviewed ten of them, but there are more, yes, many more.

Know that the precious Book of Mormon is a sign of the last days. Those who serve as missionaries are fulfilling the sign of the covenant of God to Abraham that all the nations of the world will be blessed by his seed. Latter-day Saints are custodians of the priesthood and of the gospel of Jesus Christ. They will carry that word to the world not only for the salvation of the people, but also as participants in the sign that all nations of the earth shall hear the gospel message before covenant of the Second Coming.

Chapter 16

LIFE AFTER LIFE

Some years ago I had a conversation with a book publisher who was interested in the topic of possible continuation of life after what we know as death. He asked if I could contribute stories from patients who had come close enough to death to experience the other side, and yet had survived to share those accounts. Sensing public interest in this subject, he would entitle the book *Life After Life.*

When I considered that request, I remembered many such incidents that had been whispered in confidence to me over the years. But those seemed too sacred to share in a worldly way, especially to the benefit of a commercial venture. Besides, what would be the validity of isolated stories of life after life without supporting testimonies of witnesses?

To me, much more logical and convincing would be a study of well-documented and carefully witnessed evidences of life after life. In fact, the activities of the living Christ in America followed his own resurrection from the dead. Many witnesses in many places have seen the risen Lord, before, during, and after his appearance to the Nephites. Among the recorded accounts are the following.

TO ASSOCIATES IN THE HOLY LAND

1. The first mortal person known to have seen the resurrected Savior was Mary Magdalene. (John 20:16-17.)

2. Another recorded appearance of the risen Lord was to other women (Mark 16:1; Luke 8:3), including Mary, the mother

of James; Salome, the mother of James and John; Joanna; Susanna; and many others.

3. Jesus appeared to Simon Peter, the senior apostle (1 Corinthians 15:5), who held the keys of priesthood authority on earth.

4. Later the same day, Cleopas, and presumably Luke, met the resurrected Lord while journeying on the road to Emmaus. The Savior partook of food with them. (Luke 24:30-33.)

5. He also revealed himself to the apostles in an upper room and showed them his hands and his feet. "They gave him a piece of a broiled fish, and of an honeycomb. And he . . . did eat before them." (Luke 24:42-43.)

6. Eight days after that first appearance to the apostles, Jesus came again to them. This time, skeptical Thomas was present. Christ said to Thomas, "Because thou hast seen me, thou hast believed: blessed are they that have not seen, and yet have believed." (John 20:26-29.)

7. At the Sea of Tiberias, Jesus appeared to seven of the Twelve who had fished all night and caught nothing. The Master then caused that their nets be filled with fish. Later, Peter was commanded to feed the flock of God. (John 21:1-24.)

8. Perhaps the greatest congregation to witness the risen Lord in Palestine occurred on the Mount near Galilee's shore. Here he was seen by more than five hundred brethren at once. (1 Corinthians 15:6.)

9. Later the Master again took the eleven to "a mountain where Jesus had appointed them." There he gave that endless charge to his apostles: "Go ye therefore, and teach all nations." (Matthew 28:16, 19.)

10. Then Jesus was seen by his brother James, who became one of his special disciples. (1 Corinthians 15:7.)

11. Paul added, "And last of all he was seen of me." (1 Corinthians 15:8; also Acts 9:4-5.)

12. Jesus bade farewell to the leaders of his church in Asia as he foretold prior to his ascension from the Mount of Olives:

"Ye shall be witnesses unto me . . . unto the uttermost part of the earth." (Acts 1:8; also Mark 16:19; Luke 24:50-51.)

13. When Stephen was stoned at the gate of Jerusalem, he "looked up stedfastly into heaven, and saw the glory of God, and Jesus standing on the right hand of God." (Acts 7:55.)

TO THE NEPHITES

14. The ministry of the Resurrected Lord continued with the Nephites, who lived on the Western Hemisphere. At least twenty-five hundred souls heard his voice, felt the nail marks in his hands and feet, and thrust their hands into his side. (3 Nephi 11:7-17; 17:25.) I sense that many of them wet his feet with their tears of joyous adoration.

15. Jesus ministered unto the dead in the postearthly spirit world. Peter testified that "the gospel [was] preached also to them that are dead, that they might be judged according to men in the flesh, but live according to God in the spirit." (1 Peter 4:6; also 1 Peter 3:19-21.)

John taught of this as well: "The dead shall hear the voice of the Son of God: and they that hear shall live." (John 5:25.)

In our day, additional scriptures have been added that attest to the ministry of the living Lord among the dead. (D&C 138.)

TO THE LOST TRIBES

16. From the Book of Mormon we read that Jesus was to visit the lost tribes of the house of Israel — to do for them, we presume, what he had done for others. (2 Nephi 29:13; 3 Nephi 17:4; 21:26.)

TO THOSE OF THIS DISPENSATION

17. After almost two thousand years, new witnesses to the resurrection of Jesus have added their testimonies of this transcendent truth. The Prophet Joseph Smith was visited in 1820 by God the Father and his Son, the resurrected Lord (JS–History 1:17.) Joseph saw them and heard their voices. He received a personal witness of the divine sonship of Jesus from the Father

himself, and he learned that "the Father has a body of flesh and bones as tangible as man's; the Son also." (D&C 130:22.)

18. Twelve years later, the Savior again revealed himself to Joseph Smith and Sidney Rigdon. "We saw him," they exclaimed, "even on the right hand of God; and we heard the voice bearing record that he is the Only Begotten of the Father." (D&C 76:23.)

19. On April 3, 1836, with Oliver Cowdery in the Kirtland Temple, the Prophet Joseph saw the Master once more. He wrote: "We saw the Lord standing upon the breastwork of the pulpit, before us. . . . His eyes were as a flame of fire; the hair of his head was white like the pure snow; his countenance shone above the brightness of the sun; and his voice was as the sound of the rushing of great waters, even the voice of Jehovah, saying: I am the first and the last; I am he who liveth, I am he who was slain; I am your advocate with the Father." (D&C 110:2-4.)

HIS WORK AND HIS GLORY

The resurrection of Jesus Christ is truly one of the most carefully documented events in history. I have mentioned many of those appearances, but others have been recorded.

Even more remarkable is the fact that his mission among men—the atonement, the resurrection—extends privileges of redemption from sin and a glorious resurrection to each one of us. In some marvelous way, fully comprehended only by Deity, this is his work and his glory—"to bring to pass the immortality and eternal life of man." (Moses 1:39.)

Teachers in the Church so instruct the old and the young. Sometimes the results are humorous. One leader shared this story with me:

As a little boy came home from Primary one day, his mother asked him what he had learned in class. He said, "My teacher told me that I used to be dust and that I would be dust once again. Is that true, Mommy?"

146

"Yes," the mother replied. "A scripture tells us so: 'For dust thou art, and unto dust shalt thou return.' " (Genesis 3:19.)

The little boy was amazed at this. The next morning, he was scurrying around getting ready for school, looking for his shoes. He crawled under the bed. Lo and behold, there he saw balls of dust. He ran to his mother in wonder, saying, "Oh, Mommy—somebody's under my bed, and they're either coming or going."

NATURE OF THE RESURRECTION

Compounds derived from dust—elements of the earth—are combined to make each living cell in our bodies. The miracle of the resurrection is matched only by the miracle of our creation in the first place.

No one knows precisely how two germ cells unite to make one. Nor do we know how that resulting cell multiplies and divides to make others—some to become eyes that see, ears that hear, or fingers that feel glorious things about us. Each cell contains chromosomes with thousands of genes, chemically insuring identity and independence of each individual. Our bodies undergo constant rebuilding according to genetic recipes that are uniquely ours. Each time we take a bath, we lose not only dirt but also cells dead and dying, as they are replaced by a newer crop. This process of regeneration and renewal is but prelude to the promised phenomenon and future fact of our resurrection.

"If a man die, shall he live again?" asked Job. (Job 14:14.) In faith, he answered his own question: "For I know that my redeemer liveth, and that he shall stand at the latter day upon the earth: and though after my skin worms destroy this body, yet in my flesh shall I see God." (Job 19:25-26.)

At the time of our resurrection, we shall take up our immortal tabernacles. Bodies that now age, deteriorate, and decay will no longer be subject to processes of degeneration. "This mortal must put on immortality." (1 Corinthians 15:53.)

This great priesthood power of resurrection is vested in

the Lord of this world. He taught, "All power is given unto me in heaven and in earth." (Matthew 28:18.) Though he supplicated his Father for aid at the eleventh hour, the final victory over death was earned by the Son. These are his words: "Therefore doth my Father love me, because I lay down my life, that I might take it again. No man taketh it from me, but I lay it down of myself. I have power to lay it down, and I have power to take it again. This commandment have I received of my Father." (John 10:17-18.)

This power he subtly proclaimed when he told the Jews: "Destroy this temple, and in three days I will raise it up. . . . But he spake of the temple of his body." (John 2:19, 21.)

The keys of the resurrection repose securely with our Lord and Master. He said: "I am the resurrection, and the life: he that believeth in me, though he were dead, yet shall he live: and whosoever liveth and believeth in me shall never die." (John 11:25-26.)

But obedience to the commandments of God is requisite if one is to be resurrected with a celestial body. Our challenge is to learn those commandments and abide by them.

I thank God for his Son, Jesus Christ, and for Jesus' mission in mortality and his ministry as the resurrected Lord. He brought about his own resurrection. Testimonies of thousands, from both ancient and modern times, attest to the truth that the resurrected Jesus is the Savior of mankind. He brought about a universal resurrection. "For as in Adam all die, even so in Christ shall all be made alive." (1 Corinthians 15:22.)

His sacrifice and his glory assure that "the spirit and the body shall be reunited again in its perfect form; both limb and joint shall be restored to its proper frame, even as we now are at this time." (Alma 11:43.)

Gratefully and positively, I affirm that there is life after life, first in the spirit world and then in the resurrection, for each and every one of us.

Chapter 17

MODERN PROPHETS SPEAK

Members of the First Presidency and the Quorum of the Twelve Apostles are sustained as prophets, seers, and revelators. Men of diverse backgrounds are called from the world to become special witnesses of the Lord. That transformation from work of the world to the ministry requires special power. That power must come from on high. Often the Lord has promised that blessing to those who qualify: "Unto as many as received me gave I power to do many miracles, and to become the sons of God; and even unto them that believed on my name." (D&C 45:8.)

The biographer of *President Ezra Taft Benson* recorded this event: "In the mid-fifties a young man working in Washington, D. C., became acquainted with Elder Ezra Taft Benson, then [United States] Secretary of Agriculture. After observing the Secretary function in his demanding, often controversial, post while trying to retain the dignity and deportment of an apostle, the man asked Elder Benson how he managed to handle everything. Elder Benson replied, in words to this effect, 'I work as hard as I can and do everything within my power. And I try to keep the commandments. Then I let the Lord make up the difference.' There, in a nutshell, lies the formula to President Benson's life and to his success." (Sheri L. Dew, *Ezra Taft Benson: A Biography*, pp. vii-viii.)

President Benson attributes much of his success to the power of prayer. He has written: "All through my life the counsel to depend on prayer has been prized above almost any other advice I have ever received. It has become an integral part of me—an anchor, a constant source of strength, and the basis of my knowledge of things divine." (*Come Unto Christ*, p. 27.)

Similar testimony of the power of prayer is borne by *President Gordon B. Hinckley*. When sustained in 1961 as a member of the Quorum of the Twelve, he made these remarks: "I am subdued by the confidence of the Lord's Prophet in me, and by the expressed love of these, my brethren, beside whom I feel like a pygmy. I pray for strength; I pray for help; and I pray for the faith and the will to be obedient. I think that I need—and I feel that all of us need—discipline, if this great work is to roll forward as it is ordained to do." (*Conference Report*, October 1961, pp. 115-16.)

President Thomas S. Monson also expressed the efficacy of prayer coupled with faith as a means by which power may be acquired: "The successful leader...recognizes that the greatest force in this world today is the power of God as it works through man. He takes comfort from the very real assurance that divine help can be his blessing. He is, through his faith, a believer in prayer, knowing that prayer provides power—spiritual power, and that prayer provides peace—spiritual peace. He knows and teaches...that the recognition of a power higher than man himself does not in any sense debase him; rather, it exalts him." (*Be Your Best Self*, p. 116.)

President Howard W. Hunter speaks of faith and prayer as protectors against temptation: "With faith, and prayer, and humility, and sources of strength from an eternal world, we are able to live unspotted in the midst of a world of temptation." (*Conference Report*, October 1976, p. 23.)

Elder Boyd K. Packer has described as "the choicest pearl" the opportunity to be guided by the Spirit of the Lord. He writes: "There is great power in this work, great spiritual power. The ordinary member of the Church,...having received the gift of the Holy Ghost by confirmation, can do the work of the Lord." (*That All May Be Edified*, p. 342.)

As do other Brethren, *Elder Marvin J. Ashton* adds the importance of humility: "Humility is not a weakness—it is a strength. I have often heard First Presidency members say, 'God cannot answer our prayers unless we are humble servants.' " ("A Seventy Is a Servant," special training session for the Seventies, September 29, 1987, p. 3.)

That same spirit of humility is evident in a statement of *Elder L. Tom Perry*. The power of testimony is evident in his expression: "My testimony had its roots in the teachings of two wonderful parents who believed in and lived the gospel. With that sure foundation, I have been able to add the overwhelming witness of the scriptures and the experiences of day-to-day striving to keep my activities in harmony with gospel principles. With such a foundation, it was not difficult to feel the power of the Holy Spirit burning within me that Jesus is the Christ, and that we are engaged in his work.

"How simple our testimonies become when we discover that righteous living begets happiness, and unrighteous living begets pain and sorrow.

"The greatest mystery to me in the whole plan is why I was honored to fill a position in the Council of the Twelve. As I travel to the stakes of Zion, I continually find greater talent in leadership, administration, teaching skills, speaking, and also those with more knowledge of the scriptures than I possess. My only comfort is that I cannot conceive of anyone having a stronger witness that God lives, and that Jesus is the Christ, than I have burning within my soul. This is the special witness which I feel forms within me a driving obligation to bear it to the world, in order that all men and women everywhere may have the same joy and comfort I experience in this special knowledge of the Savior." (Personal communication to the author, March 1988.)

Interestingly, *Elder David B. Haight* sounded a similar theme in a conference address: " 'I need thee; O I need thee; Every hour I need thee!' . . . The weight of this new calling and the responsibility to which you have . . . sustained me would be overwhelming were it not for my knowledge of the Savior. I have prayed daily for a deeper understanding of the Master as I prepare for this sacred responsibility." (*Conference Report*, April 1976, pp. 29-30.)

Elder James E. Faust cited his views in preparing for service to the Lord: "With faith in the Lord and humility, a priesthood leader may confidently expect divine assistance in his problems. . . . Brethren, we can learn, we can study, we can comprehend the basic things we need to know as members of God's holy priesthood. We can learn the giant truths and teach them with intelligence and understanding to those who come to learn. We can also lean upon the strengths of others whose talents are greater than our own." (*Conference Report*, October 1980, pp. 51-52.)

Elder Neal A. Maxwell also expressed the linking of humility with the obtaining of divine power: "Is there not deep humility in the omnicompetent Christ, the majestic Miracle Worker, who acknowledged, 'I can of mine own self do nothing' (John 5:30)? Jesus neither misused nor doubted his power, but he was never confused about its source, either. Instead, we mortals — perhaps even when otherwise modest — are sometimes quite willing to display our accumulated accomplishments, as if we had done it all by ourselves. Hence this sobering reminder: 'Say in thine heart, . . . remember the Lord thy God: for it is he that giveth thee power' [Deuteronomy 8:17-18]." (*BYU Speeches of the Year*, 1986-87, p. 55.)

The thoughts of *Elder Russell M. Nelson* are amply exposed in this volume and need not further be quoted in this chapter. He echoes and sustains these inpired thoughts of his esteemed associates with whom he labors in love.

Elder Dallin H. Oaks offered this profound observation regarding the unique path of preparation that preceded his calling: "As I prayed and pondered the significance of this calling, I was also filled with gratitude that our Heavenly Father would call me to this position, where I can use my experience and spend all my time for the rest of my life in his service. I have had an unusual combination of professional and Church experiences. For many years I have felt a strong sense of stewardship in respect to those experiences. I have been convinced that I was being prepared for further service. Many times I prayed that when the time came, I would be able to recognize the work for which I had been prepared, and be able to be an instrument in the hands of the Lord in performing it." (*BYU Devotional and Fireside Speeches*, 1984-85, p. 8.)

Dependence on the Lord was also stressed by *Elder M. Russell Ballard* when he was called to the Quorum of the Twelve: "I understand the source of the call. . . . This is our Heavenly Father's church. The errands that I have been sent on to act in the name of the Lord enable me to witness to you today that I know, as I know that I stand before you, that Jesus is the Christ, that he lives. He is very close to this work and very close to all of us who are asked to perform the work throughout the earth in his name." (*Conference Report*, October 1985, p. 99.)

When *Elder Joseph B. Wirthlin* was first called to be a General Authority, he summarized the roots of his faith: "My life really is anchored to the testimony that God lives, that Jesus is the Christ. I honor the priesthood that I bear, and I have seen its great power in healing the sick. I know that the Lord's Spirit does whisper to his servants, and it is up to us to listen to these whisperings." (*Ensign*, May 1975, p. 103.)

Modern prophets have spoken, each in his own way, but with themes that are essentially superimposed. These scriptures summarize so well their testimonies:

"Men should be anxiously engaged in a good cause, and do many things of their own free will, and bring to pass much righteousness; for the power is in them, wherein they are agents unto themselves." (D&C 58:27-28.)

"Those who desire in their hearts, in meekness, to warn sinners to repentance, let them be ordained unto this power. For this is a day of warning, and not a day of many words. For I, the Lord, am not to be mocked in the last days. Behold, I am from above, and my power lieth beneath." (D&C 63:57-59.)

"Thy servants may go forth from this house armed with thy power, and that thy name may be upon them, and thy glory be round about them, and thine angels have charge over them." (D&C 109:22.)

Living servants of the Lord do go forth armed with such might and power. They are mighty in speech and in spirit. What they are is the result of their continuing desire to be faithful, humble, prayerful, disciplined, and submissive servants. They are well informed regarding doctrines of Deity. Indeed they exemplify this enlightening verse of scripture: "Seek not to declare my word, but first seek to obtain my word, and then shall your tongue be loosed; then, if you desire, you shall have my Spirit and my word, yea, the power of God unto the convincing of men." (D&C 11:21.)

The potential for that divine power is within us. It awaits the grasp of each willing child of God.

BIBLIOGRAPHY

Bell, Stella Jaques. *Life History and Writings of John Jaques*. Rexburg, Idaho: Ricks College Press, 1978.

Benson, Ezra Taft. *Come Unto Christ*. Salt Lake City: Deseret Book, 1983.

Church News, weekly section of the Deseret News, Salt Lake City, Utah.

Churchill, Winston. "The Follies of the Victors" in *The Gathering Storm*. Boston: Houghton-Mifflin, 1986.

Conference Report. Proceedings of annual and semiannual general conferences of The Church of Jesus Christ of Latter-day Saints.

Cook, Lyndon B., and Andrew Ehat, eds. *Words of Joseph Smith*. Salt Lake City: Bookcraft, 1980.

Dew, Sheri L. *Ezra Taft Benson: A Biography*. Salt Lake City: Deseret Book, 1987.

Hymns, The Church of Jesus Christ of Latter-day Saints, 1985.

Kimball, Edward L., ed. *The Teachings of Spencer W. Kimball*. Salt Lake City: Bookcraft, 1982.

Monson, Thomas S. *Be Your Best Self*. Salt Lake City: Deseret Book, 1979.

Packer, Boyd K. *That All May Be Edified*. Salt Lake City: Bookcraft, 1982.

Relief Society Handbook. Salt Lake City: The Church of Jesus Christ of Latter-day Saints, 1931.

Richards, Stephen L. *Where Is Wisdom?* Salt Lake City: Deseret Book, 1955.

Smith, Joseph F. *Gospel Doctrine*. Salt Lake City: Deseret Book, 1977.

Smith, Joseph Fielding. *Doctrines of Salvation*. 3 vols. Salt Lake City: Bookcraft, 1954-56.

Smith, Joseph Fielding, comp. *Teachings of the Prophet Joseph Smith*. Salt Lake City: Deseret Book, 1976.

Widtsoe, John A., ed. *Discourses of Brigham Young*. Salt Lake City: Deseret Book, 1941, 1966.

Index

Abrahamic covenant, 136
Adaptation of the body, 7-8
Agency, obedience requires, 49. *See also* Freedom
Aging, challenges of self-mastery in, 63-64
Alcohol, effects of, 79
America, Christ appears in, 145
Anderson, Joseph, 62-63
Ashton, Marvin J., 151
Atonement: provides immortality, 23-24; act of, transcends time, 57; as a covenant, 138

Ballard, M. Russell, 153
Barriers, overcoming artificial, 85
Benson, Ezra Taft, 80, 105, 149-50
Body, human: creation of, 2-3; organs of, 3-5; backup systems of, 5; self-defense of, 5-6; self-repair of, 6-7; self-renewal of, 7; auto-regulation of, 7; adaptation of, 7-8; death of, 8-9; as a temple, 11-12; as house for the spirit, 13-14, 60; divine origin of, 33
Boyle, Robert, 51
Brain, magnificence of, 4

Chastity: leads to self-mastery, 62; in marriage, 77; as a commandment, 129-32
Children: honoring, 32; joy in, 81
Choices, importance of prayer in making, 19
Church of Jesus Christ of Latter-day Saints, embraces all truth, 36-37
Churchill, Winston, 98-99
Circumcision, covenant of, 136

Commandments, Ten. *See* Ten Commandments
Communication with God, 120-21
Companions, courtesy to, 76-77
Covenants: the rainbow, 135-36; circumcision (Abrahamic covenant), 136; the Passover, 136-37; keeping the Sabbath day holy, 137; crossing the Jordan, 137-38; the Atonement, 138-39; tokens of everlasting covenants, 139-40; the Second Coming, 140-41
Coveting, 133-34
Cowdery, Oliver, 104-5, 146
Creation: of human body, 2-3; theories of, 9; divine, 9-10; purpose of, 11-12; role of priesthood in, 108; of Eve, 108-9

Death of the body, 8-9
Deception, avoiding, 139

Earth, reasons for coming to, 123
Education: is essential for service, 30; increases faith, 33; scriptural, 51. *See also* Knowledge; Learning
Emerson, Ralph Waldo, 40
Eulogy, writing own, 29
Eve: creation of, 109; as a partner, 109-10; motherhood responsibilities of, 110; spirituality of, 110-12; kept commandments, 112-13; taught the gospel, 113-14
Evelyn, John, 51
Exercise: and self-mastery, 62-63; physical, 79

Faith: this life a test of, 16-18; in God,

157

serves as consultant to government, 95; is ordained an apostle, 105; gives blood, 112-13; takes daughters fishing, 113; discusses standards with daughter, 117-21; consoles friend, 127-28; visits China, 137; book is a testimony of, 152

Oaks, Dallin H., 132-33, 152-53
Obedience: power of, 41; definition of, 48-49; requires knowledge, 49; requires agency, 49-50; inappropriate emphasis on, 53-54; faith and, 54; to a living prophet, 55; priesthood worthiness depends upon, 104; and sacrifice, 112; is necessary for exaltation, 148
"Oh Say, What Is Truth?," 91
Organs of the body, 3-5

Packer, Boyd K., 150
Parents, honoring, 31-32, 127-29
Passover, 136-37
Pasteur, Louis, 37, 52
Perfect, definition of, 23-24
Perry, L. Tom, 151-52
Petersen, Mark E., 21
Poor, the: neglect of, 67-68; blessings promised to those who care for, 68; in Book of Mormon times, 68-69; in modern times, 69; food storage helps, 70; worthiness of, 70-71; fasting helps, 71; gospel changes attitude of, 71-73
Pornography, avoiding, 36
Power: use and misuse of, 39; to learn, 39-40; of labor, 40-41; of obedience to law, 41; of love, 41-42; spiritual, source of, 42-43; spiritual, prayer strengthens, 43; spiritual, revelation conveyed by, 43; spiritual, misuse of, 43-44. *See also* Priesthood
Prayer: importance of, in making choices, 19; importance of, in learning process, 35; strengthens spiritual power, 43; as a greeting to God, 78; testimony of, 149-50
Priesthood: spiritual power of, 43, 44; keys of, 101; in ancient days, 102; during Christ's ministry, 103; in modern times, 103-4; responsibilities of, 104; restoration of, 104-5;

role of, in creation, 108. *See also* Power
Posterity. *See* Children
Prophets: learning from, 20-21; testimonies of, 149-53

Rainbow, covenant of, 135-36
Repentance, requirements of, 11-12
Resurrection: process of, 7, 9; of Christ, 146; nature of, 147-49
Revelation conveyed by spiritual power, 43
Richards, Stephen L, 50, 95-96
Rigdon, Sidney, 146
Righteousness, joining truth with, 96-97
Role models, choosing, 35

Sabbath day, keeping holy, 60-61, 126-27, 137
Sacrifice: definition of, 45-46; ordinance of, 46-47, 112; of Isaac, 47; blood, 47-48
Samuel, disobedience to, 55-56
Satan, avoiding temptations of, 13
Scripture study: pattern for, 21-22; joy in, 78
Scriptures: teach endurance, 64; as instructions, 124; summarize testimonies, 153-54
Second Coming, covenant of, 140-41
Self-defense system of the body, 5-6
Self-esteem, 77-78, 79-80
Self-mastery: the body helps develop, 12; process of becoming involves, 23; definition of, 59; honoring the Sabbath leads to, 60-61; fasting leads to, 61; following the Word of Wisdom leads to, 61-62; chastity leads to, 62; exercise is a part of, 62-63; work and, 63; old age and, 63-64; strength in, 64-65; blessings of, 134
Self-renewal of the body, 7
Self-repair of the body, 6-7
Semmelweiss, 51
Service: to fellowmen, 30-31; joy in, 77
Shakespeare, William, 62, 91-92, 133
Signs, at birth and death of Jesus, 138-39
Silence, truth and, 95, 98-99
Sin, avoiding, 36
Smith, Joseph: ponders scriptures, 19; receives Word of Wisdom, 34, 79;

imperfection of, 37; accepting, 50;
Lord consoles, 56-57; on priesthood,
102, 108; priesthood conferred
upon, 104-5; God and Christ appear
to, 145-46
Smith, Joseph F., 19, 102
Snow, Eliza R., 57
Socrates, 36-37
Spirit, the body houses the, 13-14, 60
Spouse: honoring, 31-32; as a partner,
109-10
Standards, maintaining high, 117-21
Statue of Liberty, 15

Talents, joy in developing, 78-79
Temple, the body as, 11-12
Ten Commandments: as moral code,
124-25; first, 125; second, 125; third,

125-26; fourth, 126-27; fifth, 127-29;
sixth, 129, seventh, 129-32; eighth,
132-33; ninth, 133; tenth, 133-34
Thoughts, learning to control, 60
Tobacco, effects of, 79
Truth: search for, 89-90; absolute, 92-93;
mercy and, 94, 100; silence and, 95,
98-99; joining righteousness with,
96-97, 100; frequency of word, in
scriptures, 99

Wirthlin, Joseph B., 153
Women: responsibilities of, 109-12;
influence of, 114
Word of Wisdom, 53-54, 61-62, 79

Young, Brigham, 46, 51, 102, 108